Indranarain Ramlall

Central Bank Ratings

A New Methodology for Global Excellence

Second Edition

palgrave
macmillan

Indranarain Ramlall
University of Mauritius, Reduit
Moka, Mauritius

ISBN 978-3-030-98712-1 ISBN 978-3-030-98713-8 (eBook)
https://doi.org/10.1007/978-3-030-98713-8

This Palgrave Macmillan imprint is published by the registered company Springer Nature Switzerland AG
The registered company address is: Gewerbestrasse 11, 6330 Cham, Switzerland

Dedicated to my parents (Leelawtee and Bijayeparsad) and GOD

Preface

At the time of writing the second edition on central bank ratings, many key changes were noted in the landscape of central banking in the world. First and foremost, once again, central banks around the world were compelled to act as shock absorbers through their balance sheets following the detrimental effects of COVID-19 on the economic activities of various economies in the world. Second, central banks now consider the objective of price stability as being practically on the same footing as that of financial stability, corroborated by the presence of financial stability reports in nearly all economies in the world. Third, and perhaps the most significant change pertains to the aggressive efforts by central banks to come up with their own digital currencies in view of fighting back against private digital currencies such as bitcoins, among others. It is no wonder that the sphere of central banking represents a highly dynamic area with challenges being the normal norm.

In view of converging towards the population number of central banks, more central banks were incorporated for the second edition of the book. It is strongly believed that over time, the full number of central banks will finally be captured in our ratings, as currently, our sample size employed for the ratings is almost close to the total number of central banks in the world.

On a final note, whether it is formally agreed or not, no one can deny the blatant truth that the quality of a central bank does entail significant repercussions on the way economic activities are conducted in an economy, congruous with the notion that central bank quality can be regarded as a corollary to country risk level. Backtesting exercises carried out do confirm such state of affairs, whether for sovereign ratings or Ease of Doing Business. From that perspective, central bank ratings can be used to assess country risk.

Moka, Mauritius
January 2022

Indranarain Ramlall
Associate Professor (Dr.)

Contents

List of Figures

List of Tables

CHAPTER 1

Introduction

1.1 Introduction

The objective of this chapter is to provide the readers with a general historical and functional overview of central banking worldwide. First, the historical background of central banking is discussed. Then, the multi-dimensional tasks of central banks are considered which is then followed by the theoretical underpinnings of monetary policy. The challenges that buffet central banks' activities are also addressed. Finally, the chapter ends by laying out the motivations behind a proper ratings methodology to set the pace for excellence in central banking worldwide.

1.2 Brief History of Central Banking

In spite of the fact that central banking constitutes a rather new phenomenon in human history with some four centuries of experience, yet central banks are now deemed as important instruments of stability, spanning from monetary to financial, all-inclusive. Prior to the creation of money, man resorted towards metals such as gold as a means of transaction. Gold exhibited some very nice features such as medium of exchange and store of value. Eventually, these metals were standardized to take the form of coins. With time, paper money was created and central banks played prominent roles in ensuring price stability.

I. Ramlall, *Central Bank Ratings*,
https://doi.org/10.1007/978-3-030-98713-8_1

Many different monetary systems came to birth. Under the gold standard, central banks were able to issue money as per the value of gold they held in stock so that less focus was laid on the amount of money required to really boost the economic activities. Emphasis was laid to keep the value of money fixed to gold. Post the end of World War I, many central banks were subject to a dearth in gold stocks leading to a drift towards the gold exchange standard. Under the latter, countries simply pegged their currencies' values to gold. Much to the credit of the famous Economist in the 1950s, John Maynard Keynes, many central banks became aware of their inherent monetary policy power in influencing economic activities. This led towards the adoption of the Bretton Woods system and the collapse of the gold standard. Under the Bretton Woods system, the United States would simply peg the US dollar to gold per ounce and all other countries would then fix the value of their currencies to the US dollar. However, the Bretton Woods system became problematic as countries were not able to support their pegged currencies, all paving the way towards the floating exchange rate regime.

With time, central banks realized that money printing generated more detrimental effects than positive impacts so the rule-based approach (see Taylor, 1993) and (Clarida et al., 1998) in lieu of discretionary-based approach became the new monetary policy development. Monetary policy underwent a new era of development in 1989 when the Reserve Bank of New Zealand pioneered the inflation targeting framework in its monetary policy implementation strategy. The crux of such an approach is that it best helps to anchor inflationary expectations so that credibility is being induced along with transparency and accountability. As new risks spurted out, central banks adjusted their monetary strategies. During the US subprime crisis, some central banks resorted towards non-conventional monetary policies in the form of quantitative easing in view of scaling down the level of financial casualties. Today, modern central banking requires adherence to both monetary and financial stability, as vital ingredients, to spur economic growth.

1.3 Multi-Tasking Central Banks

Considered as the forefront actors in financial systems, central banks play preponderant roles when it comes to safeguarding the price stability function. However, with the impacts of globalization, central banks have been subject to constant pressures in view of being more flexible in terms of multi-tasking or multi-dimensional tasks. Financial systems tend to be either bank-based or market-based (see Demirgüç-Kunt & Levine, 1999). As financial systems became more integrated and sophisticated, central banks were called upon to play more critical roles such as safeguarding the health of the financial system based on their vested powers of monopoly over the issuance of currencies, reserves management and close links with the governments. The most prominent of these tasks relates to the maintenance of financial stability with proper containment of systemic risks. Unfortunately, price stability or financial stability merely constitutes one of the other attributes that characterize a sound and properly functioning central banks. For instance, a central bank may be very successful in these functions but fares badly when it comes to timely and detailed reporting of its financial statements. These financial statements are particularly vital to gauge the transparency and sound corporate governance status of a central bank (see Ingves, 2011). The objective of this book is to construct a complete set of metrics to assess all the intricate activities of central banks in the world. In essence, a unique and innovative global central banking ratings system is developed. The ratings system can be used by international authorities to leverage the quality of central bank activities in the world and thereby establish a benchmark for comparative analyses.

1.4 Theoretical Underpinnings of Monetary Policy

The most basic foundation of monetary policy relates to the quantity theory of money as captured by Fisher's (1911) equation of exchange where the product of the quantity of money and velocity in circulation is tantamount to the product of price level and the level of output generated. It is assumed that the level of output and the velocity of circulation are constants so that any rise in the quantity of money translates into an increasing price level in the long run. However, in the short run, monetary policy can be used to stimulate economic activities and scale down unemployment but at the expense of inciting higher inflation. Such a phenomenon became captured by the Phillips curve which essentially depicts an inverse relationship that subsists between unemployment and inflation. The basic intuition behind the Phillips curve relates to the ability of central banks to decide about the inflation level and then let the corresponding level of unemployment prevail. In the long run, such an inverse relationship evaporates as unemployment is stuck at its natural rate, succinctly labelled as the natural rate of unemployment and also known as the non-accelerating inflation rate of unemployment (NAIRU). With time, it came to note that NAIRU could be adjusted over the long run through structural policies. In the 1970s, a breakthrough manifested in the arena of monetary policy, usually formalized as Lucas critique[1] (1976). It came to note that monetary policy became ineffective when policymakers relied solely on historical relationships among macroeconomic variables so much so that it was deemed best to rely on rational expectations instead of adaptive expectations to shun systematic bias. Lucas' critique heavily impregnates monetary policy in today's world. Indeed, sophisticated Dynamic Stochastic General Equilibrium models obviate Lucas' critique problem by focusing on the parameters of microeconomic units. Sargent and Wallace (1976) pointed out that, based on rational expectations, change in monetary policy stance would be fully anticipated by economic units so that the full impact would be nullified, leading to policy ineffectiveness or impotency. Kydland and Prescott (1977) came up with the time inconsistency problem. They argued that monetary authorities should cling to the announced policies or stick to rules to give credibility to their policies. Bindseil (2014) comments that while monetary policy represents a rather systematic approach during normal times, during crisis conditions, monetary policy implementation constitutes more of art due to significant risks being unleashed on central banks.

1.5 Challenges Facing Central Banks

Today, central banks are subject to a myriad of challenges. A report issued by Deloitte (2011) pointed out certain, though not thorough, challenges faced by central banks such as reputational risk, accounting framework and valuation challenges, management of currencies in circulation, confidentiality versus transparency, governance and retaining people. Reputational risk is particularly demanding during stressful times such as those witnessed during the 2007 US crisis. The ability to undertake sound policies during critical times constitutes a major catalyst that shapes reputational risk. The latter is undeniably and inherently linked to credibility

[1] A somewhat similar concept to Lucas critique pertains to the Goodhart's law (1989) which states that once changes are effected on variables for control purposes, they will trail behind an irregular historical pattern in the data.

which is emphasized for countries that cling to inflation targeting strategies (see Bernanke & Mishkin, 1992; Mishkin, 2007). As the book later shows, central banks fail to adhere to consistent accounting policies as they tend to adopt their own way of reporting. Such a state of affairs was highlighted in Deloitte (2011) report as: "Many central banks are permitted by their Central Banking Act to adopt a national or global accounting standard or to develop their own specific financial reporting rules to accommodate the unique circumstances of central banks". Model risks present considerable challenges when it comes to proper valuations as history may not repeat itself of systemic shocks. Apt inventory controls should be established to ensure proper management of currency in circulation. Transparency in terms of operating activities and information constitutes an important driver for a smooth functioning central bank . Risk management of the financial system lies on the back of central banks as demonstrated by quantitative easing measures undertaken to endorse the economy. The list of challenges pointed out by Deloitte (2011) is not exhaustive as it fails to incorporate other important components such as the language of dissemination, adherence to green concept and efficiency, among others.

One of the most vital challenges which cropped up in light of the crisis pertains to proper interest rate setting. As a matter of fact, it has been observed that low interest rates were one of the main causes of the US Subprime crisis and they induced excessive borrowing well beyond the repayment capacity of borrowers. Central banks have the responsibility to thereby establish sound macroprudential policies in view of curtailing asset price increases beyond their fundamental values. Globalization also presents similar challenges as deregulation and liberalized markets instil a culture of free capital flows and movements of goods and services. These capital inflows may consolidate on speculative local asset price bubbles. Ironically, a sudden cease in capital inflows may destabilize the whole gamut of the financial system . Central banks therefore have a major role to play to shun off asset price bubbles with proper regulatory measures to ensure that excessive inflows and outflows of capital flows do not disrupt the smooth functioning of the financial system.

Capital and reserve requirements constitute the backbone of modern central banking in view of consolidating the soundness of the banking system. Since 1988, central banks clung to the capital requirement guidelines as stipulated under Basel I and issued by the Committee on Banking Supervision. The ultimate philosophy embedded in Basel I pertained to how much capital banks should maintain to cushion against distinct risks embodied in various assets so that credit risk is properly contained. To circumvent the shortcomings in Basel I, Basel II was subsequently introduced in 2004, namely to give due consideration to both liquidity and operational risks with more stress being exerted on off-site supervision activities. Post the onset of the crisis, Basel III was consequently introduced in 2010 with the introduction of three pillars and minimum global liquidity standard (liquidity coverage ratio and net stable funding ratio) and additional capital buffers for systemically important financial institutions. The objective behind reserves requirements is to ensure that banks are equipped with ample liquidity to obviate any liquidity risk situations. Despite the fact that reserve requirements constitute part of monetary policy tools, yet central banks tend to shun their uses due to considerable costs being exerted on the banks. For instance, a hike in reserve requirements ratio may compel banks to claim back their loans to have enough cash to be deposited as reserves, thereby imposing strenuous costs on both banks and their customers. Hence, maintenance of proper capital and reserve requirements constitutes an important challenge to central bankers.

Sound regulatory measures often characterize many central banks in the world. Such apt regulatory framework is heavily based on on-site and off-site examinations of banks. On-site examination relies heavily on CAMELS ratings to capture capital adequacy, asset quality, management, earnings, liquidity and sensitivity to market risks. Off-site examination refers to analysing the gleaned data to address any deficiencies.

The global financial crisis has shown that central banks' roles should not only be confined to monetary stability but should extend to incorporate financial stability and also a satisfactory dose of employment in a country. Technically speaking, monetary stability assists economic agents to effect their investment-consumption decisions in an optimal manner. For instance, a low and stable inflation rate constitutes the best mechanism to ensure confidence in an economy so that households and firms are motivated to invest and consume more. To date, there is no single definition for financial stability but it can be considered as a state where an economy is properly functioning without any disruptive forces impregnating its financial system. The need to maintain employment level during crisis times has been one of the modern roles of central banking, as witnessed during the recent crisis, in spite of the fact that full employment does not happen to fall under the purview of all central banks' mandate in the world. Overall, central banks are now subject to striking a proper balance among the trident roles of monetary stability, financial stability and a satisfactory employment level.

Perhaps among the different crises which hit the world, COVID-19 remains the most powerful crisis not only in terms of the time period it held the world at its mercy but also in terms of the degree of damage it trailed behind. Governments around the world were compelled to adopt unprecedented measures with lockdowns being the widely used strategy at the commencement of the crisis to properly contain its spread. Companies around the globe were forced to practise digitization to ensure at least minimum delivery of business services. The working environment witnessed a real blow with working from home becoming the norm of day to day lives of individuals.

As far as central banks are concerned, significant bailout packages were deployed to counteract the detrimental effects of COVID-19. In some cases, first-round and second-round packages had to be implemented based on evolving situations. Similar to the situation witnessed during the global financial crisis of 2007–2008, the balance sheets of central banks acted as shock absorbers following the launching of various asset purchase programmes. However, compared to the global financial crisis, the risk in itself was not a financial risk at source but a virus transmission risk harming human health to eventually impact the financial system through various household sector linkages. One key feature conspicuously noted during the crisis pertained to the increasing use of digitization by banks to ensure the maintenance of financial services during lockdown periods. Such a digitization state could be leveraged by central banks in view of offering digital currencies which are considered to be a highly effective way of transferring financial resources to the needy ones during crisis conditions.

1.6 Establishing a Benchmark for International Excellence in Central Banking

Based on the aforesaid challenges, it becomes *sine qua non* to set up metrics that can assess the quality of central banking worldwide. The metrics used should be holistic and capture all the important aspects of central banking. It is with this quest in mind that the book has been written. Basically, the objective is to glean, based on availability and accessibility of data, a full set of metrics that would capture the quality of operational activities of central banks in the world. Consequently, a unique and innovative ratings system is set up. The ultimate aim is to rate each central bank to thereby emerge with a sound classification in terms of rankings. The chief purpose of establishing such a global central bank rating system is to put forth a benchmark for excellence so that, with time, central banks can leverage the quality of their activities. Furthermore, and most importantly, the rating system will assist international authorities to focus more on poorly rated central banks, those found at the lower rung of the ratings ladder. It is anticipated that the newly developed ratings system will be widely used by the international authorities when it comes to gauging on quality of central banks worldwide.

Mishkin (2010) argued that in light of the US subprime crisis, monetary policy task has become more difficult on the ground for a plethora of reasons. First, monetary and financial stability are highly intertwined. Second, financial disruptions imply the need to cling to the non-linear monetary policy framework. However, Mishkin (2010) pointed out the good news in that research is like generating further refined models that will best help policymakers in devising better strategies. This will keep the stamina on monetary policy research as an ongoing field for the decade to come. It is with this excitement in mind that the current work has been undertaken in view of generating a better framework for central banking worldwide which will undeniably ricochet back on monetary policy strategies.

References

Bernanke, B. S., & Mishkin, F. S. (1992). Central bank behavior and the strategy of monetary policy: Observations from six industrialized countries. NBER Macroeconomics Annual. In O. Blanchard & S. Fischer (pp. 183–228). MIT Press.

Bindseil, U. (2014). *Monetary policy operations and the financial system*. Oxford University Press.

Clarida, R., Gertler, M., & Galí, J. (1998). Monetary policy rules in practice: Some international evidence. *European Economic Review, 42*(6), 1033–1067.

Deloitte Global Services Limited. (2011). *Key challenges facing central banks: Adapting to a new era*.

Demirgüç-Kunt, A., & Levine, R. (1999). *Bank-based and market-based financial systems: Cross-country comparisons* (Policy Research Working Paper 2143). The World Bank.

Fisher, I. (1911). *The purchasing power of money*. Macmillan.

Goodhart, C. A. E. (1989). *Money, information and uncertainty* (2nd ed.). Palgrave Macmillan.

Ingves, S. (2011). *Central Bank governance and financial stability: A study group report*. Bank for International Settlements, Basel, Switzerland.

Kydland, F. E., & Prescott, E. C. (1977). Rules rather than discretion: The inconsistency of optimal plans. *Journal of Political Economy, 85*, 473–491.

Lucas, R. (1976). Economic policy evaluation: A critique in the Phillips curve and labor markets. In K. Brunner & A. Meltzer (Eds.), *Carnegie-Rochester Conference Series on Public Policy*, 1 (pp. 19–46). American Elsevier.

Mishkin, F. S. (2007). Does inflation targeting matter? With K. Schmidt-Hebbel, in F. S. Mishkin & K. Scmidt-Hebbel (Eds.), Monetary policy under inflation targeting (pp. 291–372). Central Bank of Chile.

Mishkin, F. S. (2010). *Monetary policy strategy: lessons from the crisis*. ECB Central Banking Conference, Frankfurt.

Sargent, T., & Wallace, N. (1976, April). Rational expectations and the theory of economic policy. *Journal of Monetary Economics, 2*, 169–183.

Taylor, J. (1993). Discretion versus policy rules in practice. *Carnegie-Rochester Conference Series on Public Policy, 39*, 195–214.

CHAPTER 2

An Overview of Central Banking in the World

Central banks constitute core financial institutions usually endowed with price stability function. However, based on steadily growing sophistication of the global financial system, there are increasingly demanding requirements that central banks are expected to fulfil, thereby enlarging its functional space. This chapter focuses on the various aspects of central banks worldwide such as functions to be undertaken, monetary policy transmission mechanism channels, special drawing rights, seigniorage, currency in circulation, money supply, electronic money, currency board, structure of their income/expense components, central bank balance sheets in light of the crisis, covered bond purchase programme and special features of central banks.

2.1 Functions of Central Banks

The functions of central banks may be split into a multi-dimensional perspective as follows.

1. Maintain price stability; usually representing its mandated or core function
2. Ensure proper provision of banking services to the government-government's banker
3. Oversee the financial system to safeguard its financial stability

I. Ramlall, *Central Bank Ratings*,
https://doi.org/10.1007/978-3-030-98713-8_2

4. Fulfil the task as lender of last resort, as magnified by the recent crisis
5. Ensure smooth operations of the payments and settlement systems
6. Establish sound Business Continuity Management
7. Promote financial market developments such as establishment of proper zero coupon yield curve
8. Fight against money laundering
9. Contain systemic risks through proper macroprudential policies
10. Improve on data collection and statistical analyses
11. Induce proactive risk management of the financial system like provision of emergence liquidity assistance under exceptional circumstances as witnessed during the crisis
12. Promote sound corporate governance
13. Enhance financial literacy via regular educational programmes to boost effectiveness of the monetary policy transmission mechanisms
14. Consolidate stakeholder relationships to ensure maximum cooperation from them
15. Set up measures, procedures and policies to properly contain systemic risks
16. Mitigate dysfunctions in the foreign exchange markets
17. Regularly conduct stress testing exercises to identify vulnerabilities and subsequently undertake proactive policies
18. Correctly assess on the level of reserve requirements in view of setting up the right level of insurance for commercial banks' obligations
19. Demonstrate strong commitment towards greener activities to set the pace for commercial banks to follow suit
20. Establish and review guidelines as and when required with respect to activities such as credit activities, foreign currency open positions and large credit exposures
21. Undertake both on-site and off-site supervisions in the case supervision falls under its purview of their operations
22. Set up capital adequacy to cushion the interests of the depositors
23. Establish proper licensing requirements
24. Development of digital currencies

The above list of functions is not exhaustive. Nonetheless, price stability predominates as the major task of nearly all central banks in the world with different functions hinging on the type and stated objectives of the central bank. Research has gained momentum in light of the crisis on certain specific aspects of central banking. For instance, Aizenman and Inoue (2013) found that central banks stuck to passive maintenance of gold stocks, irrespective of the price patterns of gold. Rhee and Turdaliev (2013) assessed the transparency of monetary policy in a dynamic stochastic general equilibrium framework. They found that social welfare did not depend on the level of transparency when preferences are logarithmic in consumption or linear in leisure.

One conspicuous element noted in recent years relates to vigorous actions taken by central banks worldwide to preserve their established monopoly power when it comes to the issuance of notes and coins. No central bank wants to lose that inherently established power. Stated differently, the mushrooming of digital currencies, crypto assets or stable coins issued by private parties led to significant pressures on central banks in devising up alternative assets. Central banks fear that if people migrate to digital currencies which are not issued by them, then, their very ability to influence the economy will be lost let alone the very vested authority bestowed to them through the sole notes and coins issuance. El Salvador stands as a unique country in the world as it already migrated to bitcoin, officially accepted bitcoin as legal currency along with US dollars. For one thing which is sure, bitcoin remains a highly volatile asset which may not suit all types of users, except for fund managers coveting alternative assets as a means to diversify their portfolio.

2.2 Monetary Policy Transmission Mechanism

Monetary policy is usually analysed through its various transmission mechanisms, namely credit, exchange rate, expectations, asset price and interest rate channels. Central bankers are usually concerned about the interest rate channel as it is where their actions are most likely to spawn changes in the level of economic activities. The exchange rate channel represents a vital monetary policy channel mainly for countries clinging towards floating exchange rate regimes. The expectations channel is best controlled via high credibility as inspired by the inflation targeting framework (see Svensson, 2008). The asset price channel calls forth sophisticated and well-developed financial markets that can instantly transmit any ramifications in the monetary policy stance. The credit channel of monetary policy works through the availability of credit to market players in the economy, mostly encompassed under the bank lending and balance sheet channels. The balance sheet manifests chiefly through the value of collaterals for households and firms, which subsequently impacts their respective wealth effects. The balance sheet channel is sometimes deemed to be a corollary to the asset price channel.

The transmission mechanism of monetary policy is perhaps the key tool that any central bank can wield to influence the level of economic activities in an economy. All in all, as previously discussed, there are five transmission channels of monetary policy, namely, credit channel, asset price channel, interest rate channel, exchange rate channel and the expectations channel. While the explanations for credit channel, asset price channel, interest rate channel and exchange rate channel can be formulated in a succinctly logical approach, the expectations channel of monetary policy is tilted more towards a qualitative approach.

(a) **Expectations channel of monetary policy transmission mechanism**

Compared to the other different types of transmission channels of monetary policy, the expectations channel is based on the notion that inflationary expectations have successfully been anchored so that the inflation rate can be properly targeted. Relatedly, the overwhelmingly used tool by central banks worldwide to anchor inflationary expectations has been the adoption of inflation targeting-pioneered by the Reserve Bank of New Zealand.

(b) **Asset price channel of monetary policy transmission mechanism**

The asset price channel of monetary policy is based on the interactions between monetary policy interest rate changes and asset prices. In practice, there exists a large number of assets such as stocks, real estates and properties at large. For the sake of explanatory purposes, recourse will be made to stocks. A hike in the policy rate unleashes shifts from stocks to bank deposits as investors find it more lucrative to put their money in banks. Consequently, stock prices plummet to impound on the wealth levels of households and corporates, so much so that this engenders a squeeze in consumption and ultimate on aggregate demand, making monetary policy efficient—a contraction monetary policy effectively reducing the aggregate demand level. Apart from wealth-consumption effects, the asset price channel of monetary policy also works through the Tobin' Q medium. Fall in stock prices ultimately affects the market value of the firm as to drag down its Tobin's Q value and since the latter is related to investments, lower Tobin's Q incites lower investments, leading to undermined levels of aggregate demand.

(c) **Interest rate channel of monetary policy transmission mechanism**

The interest rate channel of monetary policy is linked to the notion that changes in interest rates directly impact both consumption and investments. For example, an increase in interest rates makes it costlier for the borrower to deter investments by corporates. In a parallel manner, a hike in policy rate induces higher savings and lower consumption as depositors refrain from current consumption to satisfy higher consumption in the future. Thus, the ultimate impact of interest rate changes on aggregate demand works through changes in both consumption and investment.

(d) **Exchange rate channel of monetary policy transmission mechanism**

The exchange rate channel focuses on how changes in policy rates eventually impact exchange rates to eventually filter down on the level of economic activities in the economy. Based on the presumption of a hike in the policy rate, this will induce foreign investors to buy more of the local currency as they switch more to local assets investment. Such an action triggers an appreciating local currency which deters exports but encourages imports, all paving the way towards lower net exports which then scale down the level of aggregate demand in the economy. Thus, the exchange rate channel of monetary policy is based on the relationship between interest rate changes, exchange rate changes, net exports and aggregate demand.

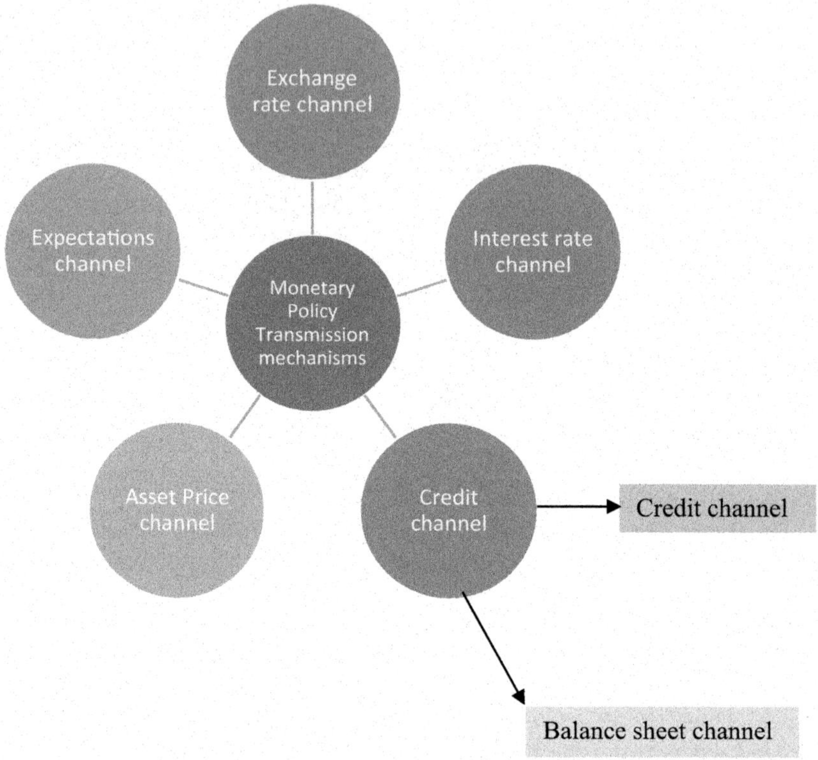

Fig. 2.1 Monetary policy transmission channels (*Source* Author's illustration)

(e) **Credit channel**

The operational mechanism of credit channel of monetary policy is dual-based, hinging on two driving forces, namely, the balance sheet channel and the bank lending channel. Under the bank lending channel, a squeeze in credit availability to borrowers effected either through price terms (higher cost of credit) or through non-price terms (collateral requirements, maturity period of loans), simply dragging down the level of borrowings as to entail subdued activities levels thereby occasioning a decline in aggregate demand level. The balance sheet channel operates through the net worth of the firms. A hike in policy rates reduces the prices of stocks and hence the market value of firms so that their net worth falls and hence banks charge higher external finance premiums rendering it costly for these firms to borrow from the banks (Fig. 2.1).

2.3 Forces That Drive Down the Transmission Mechanism of Monetary Policy

1. ***High levels of dollarization/euroization***

Under dollarization, there is little recourse towards the use of local currencies as a large component is based on US dollars so much so that the economy is subject to the vagaries of the economic state of affairs prevailing in the US. Nonetheless, dollarization constitutes the preferred choice when the foreign currency is imbued with greater stability relative to the local currency. Other benefits are attached to the use of dollarization such as greater capital inflows from the US and a reduction in currency risk mismatches. Assessing the other side of the coin, dollarization implies acceptance of foreign monetary base so that there is an automatic loss of seigniorage income which goes to the US. In the same vein, since monetary base comprises US dollars, it is not easy to control money supply leading to a loss of independence in monetary policy implementation. Parallel economic affairs prevail in the case of euroization.

2. ***Fixed exchange rate regime***

According to Mundell–Fleming theory, fiscal policy is most effective under a fixed exchange rate system while monetary policy is most potent under a floating exchange rate regime. Under a fixed exchange rate regime, the need to maintain the mandated exchange rate signifies considerable foreign exchange market interventions which eventually trail behind repercussions onto the money supply. Consider the case of a balance of payments surplus based on higher demand for a country's goods which then ricochets into higher demand for its currencies. Based on the inexorable forces of demand and supply, this is anticipated to trigger an increase in the price of the local currency vis-à-vis the foreign currency price. To maintain the peg, the country will be compelled to supply local currencies and demand foreign currencies. As the central bank supplies more local currencies in the foreign exchange market, this spawns an increase in the money supply. Hence, under a fixed exchange rate regime, any balance of payments surplus (deficit) is synonymous with an increase (decrease) in the money supply. In a nutshell, the fixed exchange rate mechanism signifies the loss of monetary policy independence with respect to the ability to control the money supply.

3. ***High levels of electronic money; this could herald the demise of central banks in the world***

Under high use of electronic money, there is low ability to physically exert control on the money supply so that central bank loses their monetary policy function. Free banking is widely applied as the concept to characterize such a type of economy whereby there is no physical flow of money with everything being done digitally.

4. ***Lack of financial market developments***

One of the crux requirements for an effective operating monetary policy relates to its ability to correctly transmit to both the money and capital markets. Indeed, to enable a fluid flow of interest rate mechanism to financial markets, there is a need to have well-developed financial markets which behave in perfect coordination with changes in monetary policy stances. This is widely captured under the asset price channel of the monetary policy transmission mechanism.

5. ***Improper coordination with fiscal policy***

Demand management policies are widely used to bring forth the desired changes to the economic performance of an economy. In the case of an inflationary gap, there is a need to cling towards contractionary policies—both on the fiscal and monetary fronts. Otherwise, if monetary policy is contractionary while fiscal policy is expansionary, there are likely to be nullifying effects, scaling down the effectiveness of monetary policy.

6. ***Structural problems***

Structural problems call forth structural solutions such as the well-known Structural Adjustment Programs, usually promulgated by the IMF. For instance, if a country is buffeted by high structural unemployment, then, labour market rigidities need to be addressed to mitigate unemployment and thereby enhance the level of economic activities.

7. ***Risk aversion level as captured by the crisis***

Despite the fact that the US adhered to Quantitative Easing, yet, inflationary pressures did not manifest as expected by many economists. Banks' failure to lend and higher risk aversion led to poor demand for money, which categorically discarded fears of inflation. Memory effects during crisis episodes generated a strong propensity to undermine credit expansion and price hikes.

2.4 Research

Research constitutes a vital task for any central bank in the world as it assists in shaping better policies. In essence, monetary policy can never work on an ad hoc basis; there is a need for solid background well-founded model to eventually assess the effectiveness of monetary policy decisions taken. This paved the way towards the Dynamic Stochastic General Equilibrium models, widely fancied by central bankers, despite the fact that the crisis undermined their roles following the emergence of liquidity traps. Cukierman (2013) points out that "Central banks' research departments may contribute to better monetary policymaking in the future, by examining changes in the quantitative relation between base money and credit to the economy..." Apart from monetary policy analysis, research is much needed in the area of econometric forecasting, stress testing exercises to identify feasible vulnerabilities, financial literacy improvement programmes, among others. It can be conjectured that research is synonymous with a sound given to an individual who is groping his way out in the dark as without research, central banks will not be able to properly wield the tools to enhance the quality of their actions.

2.5 Reserves Management

Reserves management is essential to ensure an optimal trade-off among diverging objectives of safety, liquidity and return. As a matter of fact, reserves are preponderant for central banks worldwide chiefly when it comes to shunning undesired fluctuations in exchange rates. For instance, in the year 2011, the Bank of Russia bought foreign currencies for the period spanning from January to August and sold foreign currencies for the last quarter of the same quarter to obviate sharp fluctuations in exchange rates. Similarly, reserves assist in muting illiquidity problems in the foreign exchange markets. Foreign exchange reserves also assist in hedging against currency risk that buffets external debt. Most importantly, reserves help to cushion a country against detrimental macroeconomic shocks like capital outflows. These sudden capital outflows are usually associated with euphoria towards a specific country not endorsed by solid economic fundamentals. It is widely acknowledged by central bankers that holding ample reserves help to ensure a credible and independent central bank. This explains the need to cling to high-quality assets when diversifying the reserves with security undeniably predominating over profitability. Net international reserves are also widely used to compute import cover ratios, a highly watched metric by international authorities when it comes to gauging the international repayment capacity of a country. Banco Central do Brasil obtained ISO 9001 certification in 2010 for excellence in its reserves management task through the setting up of international best practices. Other central banks are expected to follow suit in view of leveraging the quality of their reserves management.

2.6 Sterilization and Its Implications for Central Banking

As rehearsed, the monetary base can be defined as the sum of the Net Foreign Assets and Net Domestic Assets. Consequently, ramifications in either Net Foreign Assets or Net Domestic Assets trigger direct changes onto the monetary base. Sterilization is defined as a transaction initiated to restore the monetary base back to its original level.

$$\Delta NFA + \Delta NDA = \Delta M1$$

where:
NFA denotes Net Foreign Assets
NDA denotes Net Domestic Assets
M1 denotes monetary base
Δ denotes change

Should a country be subject to a deficit in its balance of payments, then, it should be experiencing a decline in its monetary base corresponding to the decline in the Net Foreign Assets, coined as the monetary approach to balance of payments. To sterilize the impact, the central bank will have to increase the monetary base by the same amount as the fall in the monetary base. This can be accomplished by bonds purchase which then elicits parallel increases in Net Domestic Assets and monetary base. However, sterilization does not manifest without any costs. First, sterilization is restrained by the extent of domestic debt market development. Countries which are buffeted by poor levels of financial developments are susceptible to experience hurdles in effectively performing their sterilization operations. Second, by buying bonds and selling foreign assets, there is an automatic squeeze on the earning capacity chiefly on ground of significant interest rate differentials between local and foreign assets. This can be detrimental in the case of a surplus running country which is then compelled to buy low-yielding foreign assets while simultaneously disposing of high-yielding domestic assets.

Sterilization can also manifest at the microeconomic level as overwhelmingly noted during the crisis. Consider the case whereby commercial banks faced substantial foreign currency outflows. The latter triggered a dearth of foreign currencies chiefly in case of foreign currency loans funded by foreign currency deposits, let alone stressful conditions in the foreign exchange market. To obviate such a problem, central banks provided the banks with the appropriate amount of foreign currencies. This drew down on the net foreign assets position of the central bank. Should these net foreign assets be funded from loans by banks or any other instruments, there would be a corresponding increase in net domestic assets of central bank. In that respect, the assets composition of the central bank changed without any modification in its size. The facility is usually provided in the form of loans granted under repo transactions which are usually secured by treasury bills.

Sterilization automatically becomes infeasible for countries that operate under currency boards like Hong Kong SAR. Basically, under a currency board, a country allows high-powered money to be generated if and only if there is an equivalent increase in foreign currency holdings.

2.7 Special Drawing Rights

Created in 1969 but launched in 1970, Special Drawing Rights (succinctly labelled as SDRs) represent the unit of account held by the International Monetary Fund. In itself, SDRs are not money because they merely represent claims on the reserves of other International Monetary Fund's members. In essence, SDRs can be exchanged for any type of foreign currency from any member of the International Monetary Fund. Though SDRs do not represent foreign currencies, yet, for accounting requirements,[1] they are deemed as foreign currencies. SDRs can only be used at international level among International Monetary Fund's members only and not for any other transactions. For example, a country cannot resort to SDR transaction in view of trading in other assets-utterly not permissible. The value of SDRs is derived from a basket of four major currencies (internationally coveted currencies), comprising of US dollar, Euro, Japanese Yen and Pound sterling. However, the components are not static as the respective weights of SDRs are reviewed every five years in light of any changes noted in international transactions. The strategy deployed behind having a basket of currencies is to significantly draw down volatilities in the value of SDRs.

To relieve its member countries from financial distress, the International Monetary Fund provides both SDRs and also Exogenous Shock Facility. SDRs constitute claims on currencies held by members of the International Monetary Fund. In light of the US crisis in 2009, the International Monetary Fund approved two versions of SDRs; a general allocation in August 2009 to all of its members to the tune of $161.2 billion in proportion to their quotas coupled with a special allocation in September 2009 of $21.5 billion. The purpose behind the crisis-induced SDRs allocations was to enshrine liquidity position at the global level. The lion's share of the general allocation went to advanced economies since they made up the most in terms of quotas. A country can increase

[1] For instance, when central banks prepare their financial statements, they convert all their SDRs into their local currency of denomination.

its SDRs levels either through direct allocations by the International Monetary Fund or via exchange of reserves in return for SDRs. Interests are remunerated to countries that exhibit SDRs holdings above cumulative SDRs allocations. Net receipt SDR countries receive interests on SDRs. In spite of the fact that SDRs exchanges can be voluntary among International Monetary Fund's members, yet, they can also be directly imposed by the International Monetary Fund. Under the Exogenous Shock Facility, the aim is geared towards enhancing the import cover of a country that has been subject to considerable negative exogenous shocks, which can surface from crisis or from structural problems.

2.8 Reasons for Holding SDRs

Many reasons prevail to push central banks to hold SDRs, namely:

1. a tool for liquidity management at the international level to mitigate global liquidity imbalances; a cheap way to increase international reserves
2. to scale down currency risk associated with foreign exchange rate fluctuations
3. ease tensions with respect to the value of international reserves
4. during the crisis, SDRs help advanced economies to help their banks which went underwater as they fail to roll-over their short-term liabilities which were mainly denominated in foreign currencies. Central banks were able to use fresh SDRs in exchange for foreign currencies that could be given to banks to offset their bruised foreign source funding base. Swap lines initiated by central banks were intended for the same purpose.

SDRs provided by IMF help needy countries to conduct macroeconomic policies without being subject to any sterilized operations which tend to be costly in nature. For instance, if a country is subject to a balance of payments deficit, this draws down on net foreign assets and thereby engenders a corresponding fall in the monetary base. To keep the monetary base intact, there is a need to boost net foreign assets or net domestic assets. Should net domestic assets be increased, this would require bond purchases by the monetary authority from local investors so that this unleashes the desired increase in monetary base. However, in case yields on foreign assets are higher than those of local assets, then, that would trigger potential losses since high-yielding returns of foreign assets have been sold in lieu of low-yielding returns of domestic assets. Should net foreign assets be increased as to reverse back its initial decline, then, SDRs can be exchanged with other IMF members for desired foreign currencies so that initial state is restored. Therefore, SDRs help countries to free themselves from undesired costs associated with sterilized operations. The interest costs associated with such SDRs exchange are likely to be low compared to the interest rate differentials between local and foreign assets. As a matter of fact, a country that gives away SDRs in exchange for foreign currencies has to pay interest on those SDRs to the IMF.

2.9 Seigniorage

Seigniorage constitutes the monetary policy bulging arm that finances the fiscal costs of the government. Seigniorage manifests out of the notes and coins monopoly issuance power of central banks. Technically speaking, seigniorage revenue is defined as the difference between the cost and the value of money. Seigniorage income is positive when the value of money exceeds its cost. There are three distinct ways to capture seigniorage as discussed by Flandreau (2006) and Buiter (2007):

i. Change in monetary base, $S_t = (\mathrm{MB}_t - \mathrm{MB}_{t-1})$
ii. Nominal interest rate times previous period monetary base; $S_t = i_t \mathrm{MB}_{t-1}$
iii. Seigniorage based on inflation tax concept; $S_t = \pi_t \mathrm{MB}_{t-1}$

S_t: Seigniorage
MB_t: Monetary base
i_t: Nominal interest rate
π_t: Inflation rate

2.10 Currency in Circulation

Currency in circulation constitutes an important metric found on the liabilities side of the balance sheet. In most cases, currency in circulation is directly measured as the sum of notes and coins issued. But, in complicated cases, currency in circulation can factor in commemorative coins, demonetized banknotes and withdrawal of banknotes. Notes tend to represent the major component of total notes and coins in circulation for all central banks in the world. Hence, a full-fledged approach to currency in circulation computation is as follows:

Notes and coins in circulation	XXX
Old banknotes withdrawn from circulation	(YY)
Demonetized banknotes	(XX)
Commemorative coins issued in circulation	XX

2.11 Definitions of Money Supply

Technically speaking, money supply is defined in dual forms; comprising of narrow money and broad money. Narrow money consists of M1 which is also defined as high-powered money or the monetary base. In its full-fledged definition, M1 comprises currency in circulation and reserves held at central bank. Both components are identified on the liabilities side of central banks' balance sheets. Broad money (M2 or above) consists of M1 and deposits such as savings deposits or time deposits. Different countries in the world tend to have distinct definitions of broad money. For instance, advanced economies tend to define money in more refined ways as to incorporate higher dimensions in their definitions such as M3 and M4.

Liabilities side definition of M1 and M2

$$M1 = \text{Currency in circulation} + \text{Reserves held in Central Bank (Demand deposits)}$$

$$M2 = M1 + \text{Savings Deposits} + \text{Time Deposits} + \text{Foreign Currency Deposits}$$

Assets side definition of M2

$$M2 = \text{Net Foreign Assets} + \text{Net Domestic Assets} + \text{Net Other Items}$$

$$\text{Net Domestic Assets} = \text{Net Claims on Private Sector}$$

$$+ \text{ Net Claims on Public Sector}$$

Quasi-Money

$$\text{Quasi-Money} = \text{Total Money Supply (liabilities side definition)} - \text{M2 (assets side definition)}$$

Broad money is also defined as a balancing component on the asset sides comprising the sum of net foreign assets and domestic assets and net other items. Indeed, as net foreign assets increase, there is an automatic rise in money supply. Domestic assets pertain to net claims of the central bank on private and public sectors, the higher the level of domestic assets and correspondingly the higher the money supply. This second definition of broad money is particularly important when assessing the main forces that drove up or down the money supply in a given economy.

2.12 Electronic Money

The European Central Bank defines electronic money as follows "electronic money is broadly defined as an electronic source of monetary value on a technical device that may be widely used for making payments to undertakings other than the issuer without necessarily involving bank accounts in the transaction, but acting as a prepaid bearer instrument".

Benefits of electronic money:

1. Induces transnational transactions to bring forth significant efficiency in the international payments—a push to international trade
2. Encourages financial assets to be kept in digitized form so that banking and custodial services become very cheap
3. Stimulates self-administered banking as to scale up the quality of information to thereby undermine any feasible financial instability risks
4. Induces safety as there is no need to keep solid money for payments
5. Promotes transparency and free banking
6. Instills a greater sense of financial stability as electronic money relies on high information quality which inherently reduces systemic risk and correspondingly lower financial system risks

7. Contagion risks are also well contained under electronic money based on the fact that electronic money dissipates financial interdependence among financial institutions
8. Scales down costs associated with payments and settlement system

The main expected radical ramification brought about by electronic money pertains to the possible demise of the role of central banks by virtue of the fact that electronic money altogether changes the functions of money, inducing free banking. In a parallel manner, the notion of seigniorage income is anticipated to sink into oblivion, should electronic money undergo mounting momentum in the decades to come.

The concept of digital money seems to be more in vogue nowadays than e-money though there is not so much of an iota of difference between them. More specifically, central bank digital currencies appear as the most widely employed term to reflect the ongoing transition of central banks towards digital currencies.

2.13 Currency Board

A currency board, also known as hard currency arrangement, constitutes an important aspect of foreign exchange arrangement. Under currency boards, there is no scope for price adjustments whether on the exchange rate side, inflation side or interest rate side; only adjustments are done via the quantity of money supply. This is what happened to Hong Kong, which had no choice but to follow the US monetary easing in light of the crisis, by scaling up its money supply. The following features usually characterize currency boards.

- Unlimited convertibility of local currency with the pegged currency
- Sacrifice of monetary policy, i.e. interest rate and inflation should be aligned to those of the pegged currency
- Central bank objectives become less important than the exchange rate target
- Absence of printing press system, i.e. money cannot be printed, rendering debt monetization difficult
- The main benefit is that currency risk becomes practically nil with respect to the pegged currency

2.14 Income/Expense Components of Central Banks

Central banks source their profits both from interest and non-interest components.

Interest income/expense

- Interests on investments
- Interest expense on deposits
- Interest income from loans
- Interest on securities in international institutions

Non-interest income/expense

- Foreign exchange gains/losses
- Commission income/expense
- Dividends paid/received

Fees and commissions income/expense

- Cash collection fees
- Customer service fees
- Custodial services
- Fees to external asset managers

Operating costs

- Staff costs
- Depreciation/Amortization

2.15 Central Bank Balance Sheets in Light of the Crisis

Many studies have been conducted in the area of financial stability and central banking. Borio (2011) and Posner (2009) argued that monetary and financial stability are intertwined in the long run. Central banks should be careful when they wield their monetary policy strategies. The existence of information asymmetry, in the form of adverse selection and moral hazard, constitutes a channel for the existence of financial stability risks. This has been explored in classical papers such as Akerloff (1970) and the more applied works of Stiglitz and Weiss (1981).

Bernanke and Gertler (1990), Fisher (1933), Minsky (1986), Gurley and Shaw (1955) and Kindleberger (1978) pointed out the intricate feedback effects that prevailed between real and financial activities. For instance, strong and rapid growth in asset and credit prices engender higher investment and consumption which then ricochet back onto the asset and credit prices, paving the way towards potential asset and credit price bubbles. Consequently, proper checks should be established to avoid price bubbles. Minsky (1986) focused on an instability hypothesis trigged by three-pronged effects of hedge financing, speculative financing and ponzi financing which culminate into a crisis. Gurley and Shaw (1955) argued that central banks need to exert effective controls over nonmoney financial assets in addition to control over money supply to ensure financial stability.

Diamond and Dybvig (1983) and Allen and Gale (2000) focused on bank runs as the causes of financial instability with systemic risk emanating from inter-linkages among different financial institutions. Resolutions, deposit insurance scheme and proper containment of systemic risks constitute the different avenues to deal with such causes of financial instability.

The recent crisis saw the widespread use of unconventional monetary policy strategy. By default, unconventional monetary policy (Quantitative Easing) transforms central banks' balance sheets as the principal shock absorber. Unconventional monetary policy automatically calls for ramifications in the components of central bank balance sheets; all having the aim to safeguard financial system stability by unleashing low borrowing costs and spurring credit expansion but at the expense of larger quasi-fiscal effects. In essence, causalities unleashed to the financial system by the crisis, generated systematic central bank balance sheet adjustments which eventually seeped into public debt—mere transformation of private sector debt problems into public debt problems. Central bank balance sheets are deemed as strategic economic instruments wielded by governments worldwide in view of obviating any decline in real economic activities.

Table 2.1 Marks assigned to credit ratings notch

AAA: 22	BBB: 14	CCC+ : 6
AA+ : 21	BBB-: 13	CCC: 5
AA: 20	BB+ : 12	CCC−: 4
AA−: 19	BB: 11	CC: 3
A+ : 18	BB-: 10	C: 2
A: 17	B+ : 9	D: 1
A−: 16	B: 8	NR[a]: 0
BBB+ : 15	B−: 7	

[a]No marks are given in the case of not rated countries

Chen et al. (2012)[2] addressed the interest rate channel, portfolio channel and expectations channel with respect to the quantitative easing adopted by the Federal Reserve bank. The portfolio rebalancing effects operated through changes in both the size and composition of private sector asset holdings. The portfolio rebalancing impacts manifested through low treasury bond and corporate bond yields in the US, which then unleashed higher capital inflows to Hong Kong and Brazil based on accentuated interest rate differentials. The interest rate channel reduced long-term yields to stimulate borrowing and spending. The expectations channel focused on a specific future policy path in view of inducing confidence. Chen et al. (2012) used a global vector error correction model to find that Quantitative Easing undertaken by Federal Reserve triggered vital cross-border effects on emerging Asia. Evidence is found in favour of an increase in bank credit and equity prices in Hong Kong and Thailand, let alone robust currency appreciation in Brazil (Table 2.1).

The crisis induced considerable focus on central bank balance sheets which underwent changes in both their size and composition. As financial institutions bore the brunt of the crisis, central banks came forward with asset purchases to ensure proper credit flows. These asset purchases undermined the assets value of central banks with corresponding downward stress exerted on their equity components. Weak equity-based central banks constituted a hitch to central bank independence by compromising on the proper conduct of monetary policy. Moreover, significant central bank balance sheets expansion signified looming inflationary risks. Indeed asset purchases led to corresponding rise in monetary base which then

[2] A chapter in Are central bank balance sheets in Asia too large?, 2012, vol. 66, pp 220–264 from Bank for International Settlements.

induced larger dose of money chasing too few goods. Hopefully, despite burgeoning monetary base, no inflation occurred. Besides, an interest rate transmission effect manifested in Asian countries as asset purchases by Federal Reserve led to low US yields which incite higher net interest rate differentials with Asian countries to boost massive capital inflows into Asian economies. Indeed, US Quantitative Easing policy affected emerging economies on the back of the US term structure of interest rate which provided a global benchmark for the pricing of international assets.

Quantitative Easing represents unconventional monetary policy as to impound on central bank balance sheets. Under Quantitative Easing, asset purchases by central banks triggered bearish trends on the yield curve. The rationale is that as the central banks purchased securities from the banks, the latter availed of higher reserves held at central bank. Subsequently, the treasury yield curve flattened out.

2.16 Covered Bond Purchase Programme

The European Financial Stability Facility was created in 2010 with the stipulated mandate to secure financial stability in Europe by unleashing financial assistance to its members, as and when required. The European Financial Stability Facility was then replaced by the European Stability Mechanism, under the same onus of consolidating financial system stability. The aim of the Covered Bond Purchase Programme, which manifested twice, namely under CBPP1 (June 2010) and CBPP2 (October 2011), was intended to buy euro-denominated covered bonds issued in the euro area to give a dose of fresh air in the funding needs of the banks. Both programmes were approved by the Governing Council of ECB.

2.17 Special Central Bank Features

1. Not all central banks report in English such as the central banks of Haiti and Madagascar. Some central banks even resort towards their own locally spoken language when reporting without using any internationally recognized language.
2. Not all central banks supervise commercial banks like UK, Australia and Japan. These systems are sometimes labelled as Twin peaks.

3. Czech National Bank provides very good stress testing coverage results, the best so far compared to any other central bank in the world.
4. By default, central banks in the world are exempt from taxes. However, some central banks do pay taxes; example includes the case when a subsidiary part of a central bank is liable to tax payments.
5. Central banks constitute the only financial institutions in the world that can operate even under negative equity. For instance, the Czech National Bank and Central Bank of Chile operate under negative equity. Such a statement can be substantiated by the comments made by Jaime Caruana in the forward part of the BIS paper by Archer and Moser-Boehm (2013) where he stated that "most central banks could lose enough money to drive their equity negative, and still continue to function completely successfully". Nonetheless, at some point in time, there will be the need to internalize the negative financial conditions of the central bank in the form of fiscal equity transfusion. However, that would undeniably increase the costs of public debt. For instance, the Ministry of Finance of the Republic of Azerbaijan contributed new capital to its central bank to offset its deficit and thereby enshrine the credibility of its central bank.
6. Most central banks tend to invest in foreign assets though there are exceptions like the central bank of Malawi which has its assets mainly tilted towards local investments in lieu of foreign investments.
7. Technically speaking, notes and coins should be found on the liabilities side of central banks' balance sheets. Nonetheless, there are exceptional cases when they appear on the assets side when they are still in production/distribution process but not yet issued to the general public.
8. Certain central banks are particularly serious in contacts. For instance, in the case of the central bank of Lithuania, there is a verification requirement prior to getting the email address for contact.
9. The Federal Reserve Bank was created in 1913 with the Federal Reserve Board located in Washington, DC, and its twelve regional

Federal Reserve banks situated in Atlanta, Boston, Chicago, Cleveland, Dallas, Kansas City, Minneapolis, New York, Philadelphia, Richmond, San Francisco and Saint Louis.

10. Central banks usually share the same mandate of price stability though certain adopt a more encompassing mandate that also incorporates full employment like in the case of the Federal Reserve Bank. Besides, crisis management task has become an inherent function of central banks worldwide following the US Subprime crisis that buffeted many countries. This can be glaringly captured by the widespread issuance of financial stability reports.
11. A cash flow statement is usually not required for a central bank as the latter can autonomously create money. Nonetheless, cash flow statement serves to unleash vital information in the operations of a central bank.
12. Should electronic money witness considerable momentum in the decades to come, this can generate the disappearance of central banks—setting the platform for free banking.
13. There is no "one-size-fits all" supervisory framework that can be applied to all countries in the world since each country is endowed with different types of financial architectures having different levels of complexity and innovation.
14. The subscribers to the capital of the European Central Bank consist of the National Central Banks of the European System of Central Banks. Germany, France and Italy account for more than 60 per cent of the total subscribed capital of European Central Bank based on the fact that the capital of each National Central Bank is computed in the proportion of each member's GDP to the total GDP of the European Union. The total capital of European Central Bank comprises both euro area and non-euro area National Central Banks.
15. Central banking constitutes more of an art rather than a science. Policies taken need to be well-calculated likewise the balls wielded by a juggler.
16. Five conditions are prerequisites for effective implementation of monetary policy. First, the problem under focus should not fall under structural problems. Second, the country is imbued with well-developed money and capital markets. Third, monetary policy should be well-coordinated with fiscal policy to ensure the maximum possible desired impact on real activities. Fourth, there

is low use of electronic money. Fifth, there are no elements of dollarization or euroization.

17. Last but not the least, the financial stability report published by the Central Bank of Malaysia is highly illustrative and very resourceful in terms of knowledge in the sphere of financial stability analysis.

2.17.1 COVID-19 and Central Banking

Central banks around the world adopted different policies to combat the harmful effects triggered by COVID-19. The National Bank of Poland bought Treasury bonds and securities in 2020 guaranteed by the Treasury under structural open mark operations in view of buttressing the liquidity of the banking sector. Coupled with the latter, currency in circulation went up on the back of heightened demand for cash under storing and precautionary needs propelled by COVID-19. Moreover, interest rates and minimum reserve rate were lowered to induce higher economic activities during the pandemic. In March 2020, the Governing Council of the ECB launched Pandemic Emergency Purchase Programme (a new asset purchase programme) with an envelope of €750 bn to combat the pandemic. COVID-19 entailed both increases and decreases in expenses. For instance, the central bank of Portugal reported decreases in expenses related to travelling expenses of staff, overtime, electricity and water consumption, travel and accommodation, and events and training. Assessing the other side of the coin, hikes in expenses were noted in the case of information systems for remote working and for personal protective equipment and sanitization materials. Along the same lines, the central bank of Luxembourg stated expenses incurred from teleworking system for staff and acquisition of masks were lower relative to savings posted from non-incurred expenses during COVID-19 such as travel, meeting and training expenses. Riksbank (central bank of Sweden) bought securities comprising a covered mortgage bond, government bonds, corporate bonds and commercial paper up to SEK 700 bn in 2020 to mute down any COVID-19 economic slowdown. The Croatian National Bank resorted to an arsenal of tools to fight the effects of COVID-19, namely, reduction in interest rates, granting of loans, asset purchase programmes and other measures to safeguard the liquidity and stability of the financial system.

Albania simultaneously experienced two shocks in 2020, namely, an earthquake and COVID-19 so much so that the central bank requested funding from the IMF on behalf of the government to the tune of SDR 139 million, amount of which corresponded to the purchase of 100 per cent of Albania's quota under the Rapid Financing Instrument (RFI).

References

Aizenman, J., & Inoue, K. (2013). Central banks and gold puzzles. *Journal of the Japanese and International Economies, 28*, 69–90.

Akerloff, G. G. (1970). The market for 'Lemons': Quality uncertainty and the market mechanism. *The Quarterly Journal of Economics, 84*(3), 488–500.

Allen, F., & Gale, D. (2000). Financial contagion. *Journal of Political Economy, 108*(1), 1–33.

Archer, D., & Moser-Boehm, P. (2013). *Central bank finances* (BIS Papers No. 71).

Bernanke, B. S., & Gertler, M. (1990, February). Financial fragility and economic performance. *Quarterly Journal of Economics, 105*, 87–114.

Borio, C. (2011). *Rediscovering the macroeconomic roots of financial stability policy: Journey, challenges and a way forward* (BIS Working Paper no. 354).

Buiter, W. H. (2007). "Seigniorage," economics—The open-access, open-assessment e-journal. *Kiel InstituTe for the World Economy, 1*, 1–49.

Chen, Q., Filardo, A., He, D., & Zhu, F. (2012). *The impact of central bank balance sheet policies on the emerging economies* (BIS Paper 66).

Cukierman, A. (2013). Monetary policy and institutions before, during and after the global financial crisis. *Journal of Financial Stability, 9*(3), 373–384.

Diamond, D. W., & Dybvig, P. H. (1983). Bank runs, deposit insurance, and liquidity. *Journal of Political Economy, 91*(3), 401–419.

Fisher, I. (1933). The debt-deflation theory of great depressions. *Econometrica, 1*, 337–357.

Flandreau, M. (2006). The logic of compromise: Monetary bargaining in Austria-Hungary, 1867 1913. *European Review of Economic History, Cambridge University Press, 10*(01), 3–33.

Gurley, J. G., & Shaw, E. S. (1955). Financial aspects of economic development. *American Economic Review, 45*(4), 515–538.

Kindleberger, C. P. (1978). *Manias, panics and crashes: A history of financial crises*. Wiley.

Minsky, H. P. (1986). *Stabilizing an unstable economy*. Yale University Press.

Posner, R. A. (2009). Underlying causes of the financial crisis of 2008–2009. New directions in financial services regulation. In R. B. Porter, R. R. Glauber, & T. J. Healey. MIT Press.

Rhee, H. J., & Turdaliev, N. (2013). Central bank transparency. Does it matter? *International Review of Economics and Finance, 27*, 183–197.

Stiglitz, J. E., & Weiss, A. (1981). Credit rationing in markets with imperfect information. *The American Economic Review, 71*(3), 393–410.

Svensson, L. E. O. (2008). Inflation targeting. In S. N. Durlauf & L. E. Blume (Eds.), *The new Palgrave dictionary of economics* (2nd ed.). Palgrave Macmillan.

CHAPTER 3

Some Stylized Facts About Central Banks

3.1 Introduction

A three-pronged approach to central bank classification is used in the current study. Central banks which display the full version of their financials in their annual reports in an international language (English or French) are classified in the excellence division. Compared to the first edition of the book, the second edition now includes ten more central banks in the analysis, namely, Argentina, Burundi, Congo, Jordan, Liberia, Maldives, Morocco, Sierra Leone, Swaziland and Zimbabwe. Central banks which have their websites either in English or French but no presence of a full version of their financials are rated in category B. Finally, central banks which do not present their websites in either English or French or do not have an active website, are rated in category C. Based on the sample of central banks classified under excellence division, further investigations are entertained with respect to the financial reporting period, age of central banks, accounting body used, continental composition of central banks and dissemination of information with respect to risk management. The ratings adopted are applied on central banks identified in the excellence division.

I. Ramlall, *Central Bank Ratings*,
https://doi.org/10.1007/978-3-030-98713-8_3

3.2 End of Period Reporting of Financial Statements

Most central banks in the world close their financials reporting period in December, aligned to end of year periods. 10 and 6 per cent of the sample report in June and March, respectively. Only a few central banks report in September, July and February. Overall, December predominates as the most coveted reporting period for financials clung by central banks in the world. It can be conjectured that December constitutes a strategic time period as central banks can attempt to do financial year adjustments in view of ensuring a comfortable level of return. For example, individual investors tend to channel a larger bunk of their income in investments when bonuses are paid in December. Though central banks can operate under negative equity, nonetheless, a decent level of profits is particularly preponderant to consolidate their credibility and independence, two prerequisite conditions when it comes to anchoring inflationary expectations (Fig. 3.1).

3.3 Continental Classification of Central Banks

Under the excellence division of central bank classification, there is a well-diversified level of central banks across diverse continents. Most of the central banks are tilted towards the European continent, trailed behind by Asia, Africa, America, Australia and others. The latter is used chiefly when a country is located in more than one continent. It is interesting to gain insight into the general decomposition of central banks all over the world as it unleashes information about the significance of central banking across each geographical segment of the globe. The greater number of central banks witnessed in Europe is due to a larger number of European countries reporting on central bank data than Asian or African countries. This can also signify greater transparency, higher accountability and transparency levels that impregnate Europe relative to Asia or Africa, chiefly when the latter tends to be plagued by high corruption and underdevelopment levels (Fig. 3.2).

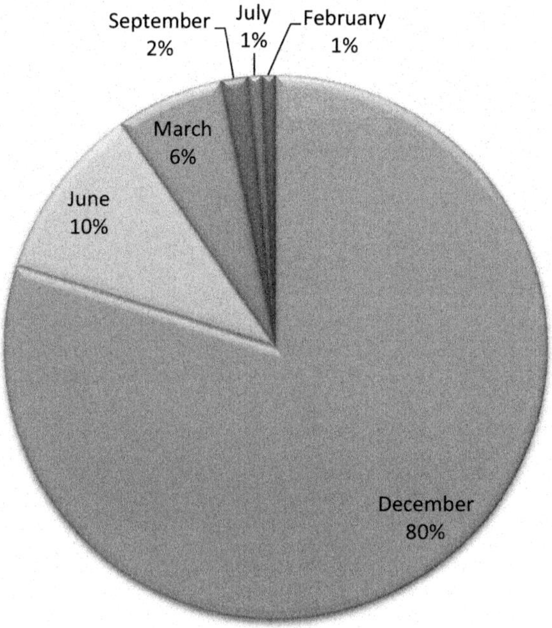

Fig. 3.1 End of year reporting of financial statements

3.4 Risk Management

Central banks worldwide are endowed with vital responsibilities as they not only ensure price stability but also safeguard the financial stability of their respective economies. Indeed, post the onset of the US Subprime crisis, there have been renewed efforts to publish financial stability reports. Unfortunately, not all central banks publish financial stability reports. In a parallel manner, risk management constitutes an ingrained function of any financial institution. Full risk management reporting pertains to full information dissemination on credit risk, liquidity risk, currency risk and interest rate risk. Some risk management reporting refers to partial reporting of the above-mentioned risks. Unfortunately, most central banks in the world do not provide full disclosure of their risks. Such a finding is vital for policymakers as it blatantly shows the need to have a well-defined risk management reporting framework for central banks in the world, bearing in mind their crucial functions. Merely 18

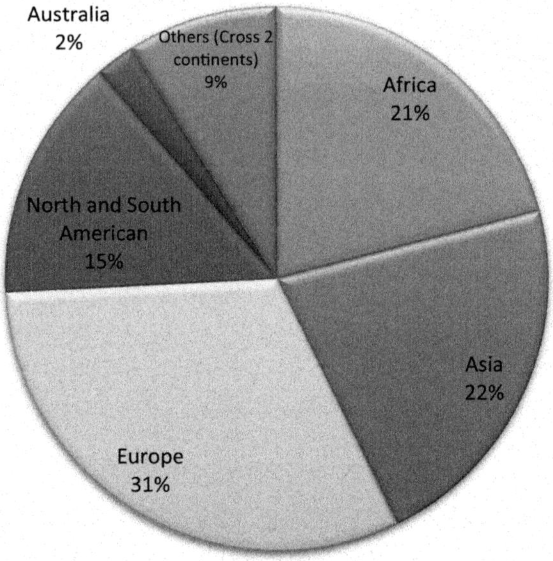

Fig. 3.2 Continental composition of central banks

per cent of central banks found in excellence division undertake full risks reporting. A priori, liquidity risk is anticipated to be of minor significance to any central bank in light of its sole notes and coins vested power. However, abuse of notes and coins issuance can spawn high inflation which self-defeats its core function of price stability. Based on the fact that a large number of central banks do not engage in full risk reporting, it is recommended that international authorities call forth a new international standard for central bank reporting to ensure both consistency and full coverage of risks in their reports (Figs. 3.3, 3.4, 3.5, and 3.6).

The age composition of central banks shows wide disparities for the distinct countries under consideration. The closing period pertains to December 2018. The horizontal axis captures the age of the central bank. While the youngest central bank in the world is Iraq, the oldest central bank is the Sveriges Riksbank—central bank of Sweden. Due to many countries considered, the age composition is illustrated in three distinct figures, low base, middle base and upper base. These three bases start off from the youngest central bank to then drift towards the eldest central banks in the world.

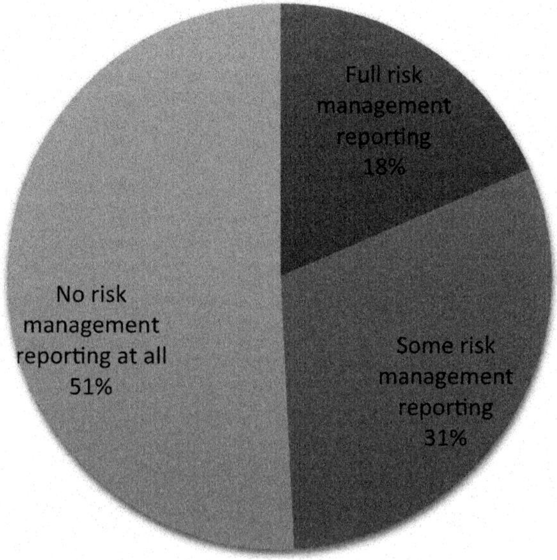

Fig. 3.3 Risk management reporting of central banks

3.5 Accounting Body

The quality of information, furnished by any institution in the world, hinges heavily on the quality of the accounting body used. It is therefore important to gauge the accounting body used by central banks. Findings show that a quarter of the central banks resorts towards KPMG as their preferred accounting body. Deloitte & Touche and PricewaterhouseCoopers share more or less the second place to the tune of 18 per cent market share. Interestingly, 22 per cent of central banks in the world do not cling to any professionally recognized accounting body, questioning the quality of their disseminated financials. Such a result signifies that international authorities should see to it that there is a general consensus as to the accounting body selected when it comes to dissemination of central bank financials to ensure that there is integrity, transparency and full disclosure of all vital information. Otherwise, window dressings are susceptible to manifest as to distort the quality of central bank financials. Overall, this boils down to the general question of who monitors central banks in the world and which institution ensures that central banks are

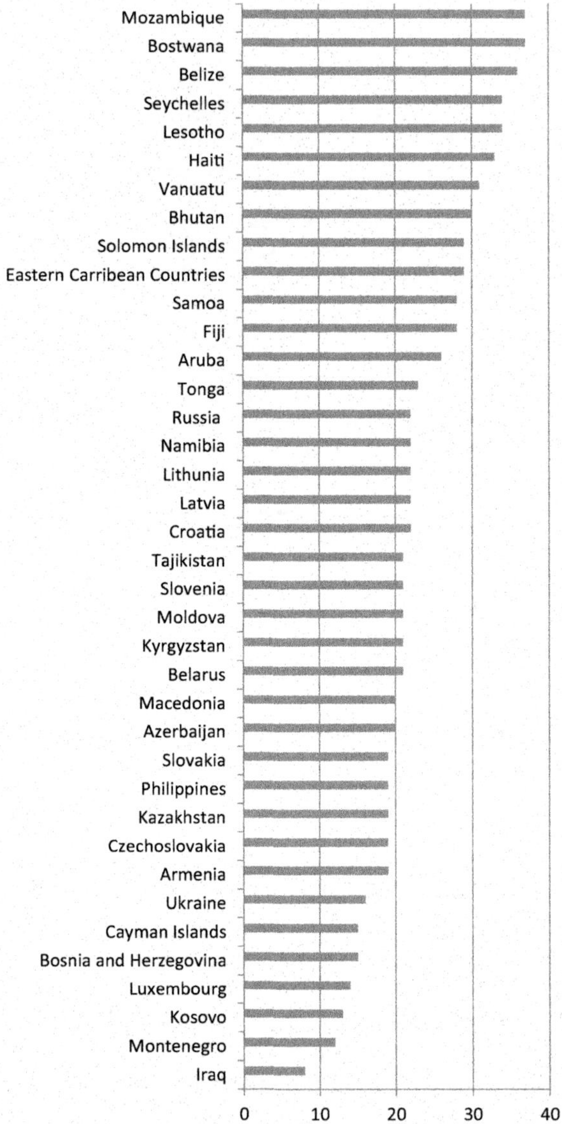

Fig. 3.4 Age composition of central banks—Lower batch

Fig. 3.5 Age composition of central banks—Middle batch

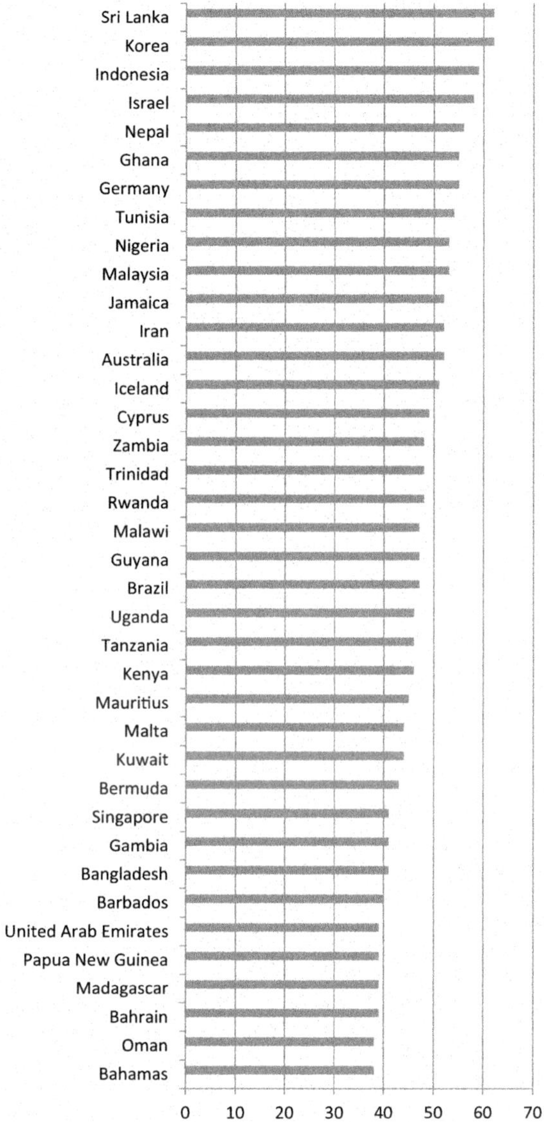

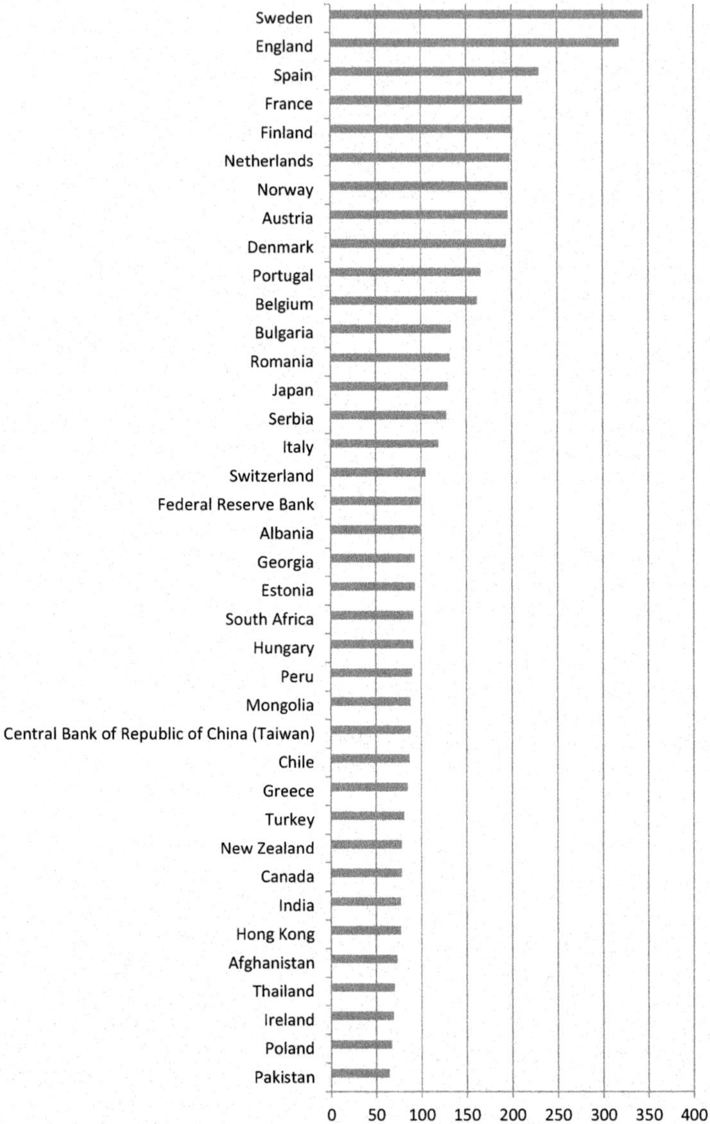

Fig. 3.6 Age composition of central banks—Higher batch

reporting sound and reliable information. Such a finding consolidates the fact that information asymmetry constitutes a major hurdle in the world despite advancements in technology.

Besides, since a quarter of central banks in the world selects KPMG, there is likelihood of KPMG having access to critical information such as coveted assets by central banks under their reserve management tasks so much so that KPMG avails of the general "herd behaviour" at the global level. This manifests out of the massive investments force of central banks so that KPMG can easily sieve out the likely effects of central bank actions on prices of world major assets. In essence, this finding clearly shows the need to put it proper monitoring mechanism by world authorities to shun away from any strategic information held by accounting bodies when dealing with central banks' financials. Unfortunately, to date, nothing concrete is established in this sphere of central banking activities (Fig. 3.7).

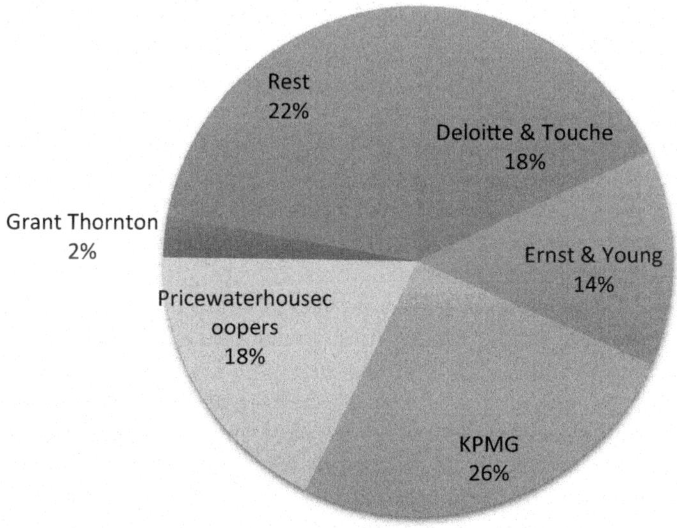

Fig. 3.7 Accounting body for central banks

3.6 Central Bank Digital Currencies

It is no wonder that central banks around the world will have no choice but to consider the adoption of central bank digital currencies to be aligned to the evolutionary state of the global financial system. This is related to the maintenance of central banks' sole notes and coins issuance power in the form of bits and bytes. Many benefits have been associated with Central Bank Digital Currencies (CBDCs). At the outset, CBDCs are expected to render monetary policy more effective in the case of interest-bearing CBDCs directly impound on different sectors of the economy. In addition, CBDCs are likely to scale down the costs of transactions, inducing enhanced levels of economic activities to spur higher levels of economic growth, as put forward by Barrdear and Kumhof (2021). Moreover, CBDCs are anticipated to bolster economic growth by promoting a formalization of the informal sector. Furthermore, cross-border CBDCs are likely to scale down transaction costs to stimulate sustainable economic growth. The last but not the least, there is widespread consensus among policymakers that CBDCs will assist central banks in effecting out "helicopter drop" where money directly flows to targeted segments of the population making central bank interventions highly effective.

However, the road is bumpy with respect to the adoption of CBDCs. It has been argued that the adoption of CBDCs can entail bank runs as people switch away from bank deposits to CBDCs, as discussed by Kumhof and Noone (2021). The very implementation of CBDCs requires a lot of investments in IT infrastructures, the costs of which can be made to be borne by taxpayers as governments embark on CBDCs. There is the feasibility that the market penetration under CBDCs is low on the back of the existence of alternative modes of digital currencies that customers already like to use such as Paytm in India and WeChat and Alipay in China. Probing deeper, there is widespread apprehension as to whether the focus will be tilted towards anonymity or traceability. Should the former predominates, then, this can make it difficult to ensure targeted portions of the population receive money flows during crisis conditions. Moreover, it could be that, at the end of the day, the tug-of-war manifests between central banks and banks. Under CBDCs, central banks yearn to retain their sole notes and issuance power while banks strive to ensure that their financial intermediation tasks are not being impeded so much so that banks can directly favour non-CBDCs forms of digital currencies should CBDCs hurt at the very survival of banks. Last but not the least, the adoption of CBDCs across borders may incite substantial spillover effects which can be outside the control horizon of central banks as to trigger upside risks to financial stability.

As of date, many central banks are still in the experimental or research phase of CBDCs with few central banks embarking on the launching process so that our ratings do not concretely factor these elements. As the horizon becomes clearer in terms of adopted CBDCs and research-based CBDCs, the ratings process will be adjusted accordingly. Nonetheless, keen readers can consult the following website[1] to get more information about the updated status with respect to CBDCs adoption worldwide. As per the website, as of date, only nine countries have launched CBDCs, namely, The Bahamas, Nigeria and seven countries in Eastern Caribbean.

References

Barrdear, J., & Kumhof, M. (2021). The macroeconomics of central bank digital currencies. *Journal of Economic Dynamics and Control, 71*, 104–148.

Kumhof, M., & Noone, C. (2021). Central bank digital currencies-design principles for financial stability. *Economic Analysis and Policy, 71*, 553–572.

[1] https://www.atlanticcouncil.org/cbdctracker/.

CHAPTER 4

Ratings Methodology for Central Banks Worldwide

4.1 Introduction

Different types of ratings have been developed in view of generating excellence in the specific area under focus. Ironically, every human being has been rated in his life based on exams undertaken at various levels of the educational pyramid. The interesting thing about rating is that it is inherently linked to a relative concept—the winner being ranked relative to any other unit in the rating scale adopted. This chapter develops the ratings methodology for central banks in the world. The chapter is split into four major sections. Section 4.2 focusses on the importance of ratings. Section 4.3 provides an overview of the institutional differences between the European Union and the US with respect to central banking. Section 4.4 discusses each of the metrics used in developing the global central bank rating methodology. Finally, Sect. 4.5 deals with the markings/scorings system of central banks based on the defined ratings methodology clung by the author.

4.2 Significance of Ratings

Many studies have been undertaken in view of generating sound rankings for policymakers such as governance assessments. La Porta et al. (1998) constructed an index of shareholder protections for the whole world to find that it correlated with economic growth and market capitalization.

I. Ramlall, *Central Bank Ratings*,
https://doi.org/10.1007/978-3-030-98713-8_4

Gompers et al. (2003) built a governance score, labelled as the G-score, to find that better-governed firms experienced superior future shareholder returns. In a parallel manner, Ashbaugh-Skaife et al. (2006) found that the higher governance ratings of GovernanceMetrics International were related to lower cost of equity. However, a study carried out by Daines et al. (2010) showed that the commercially available corporate governance rankings under The Corporate Library, GovernanceMetrics International and Institutional Shareholder Services Inc. did not generate useful information for shareholders. Furthermore, Daines et al. (2010) provided a clear demarcation line between academic and commercial indices. They argued that commercial governance ratings are more reliable and valid relative to academic indices/ratings based on the following features, namely, commercial success, use of high-quality quantitative algorithms built by experts while academic indices are constructed based on a good or bad governance mechanism, rating of each firm relative to peers, due consideration being given to market trends and the use of large database. Based on the ratings from The Corporate Library, Institutional Shareholder Services and GovernanceMetrics International and Standard & Poor's, Ertugrul and Hedge (2009) found that corporate governance ratings were poor predictors of future firm performance. Brown and Caylor (2006) built a governance score by using the Institutional Shareholder Services Inc. governance components to find an inverse relationship between governance scores and return on equity. In addition, Gompers et al. (2003) constructed a governance index (G-index) to find that firms, which were subjected to poor shareholder rights, exhibited lower stock returns and firm valuations. Ratings have also been applied in the insurance sector as studied by Pottier (1997) and Best (1992), who rated insurance companies based on a set of both qualitative and quantitative forces to generate an opinion of the company's strength in honouring the obligations of the policyholders. Best (1992) found that insolvency rates plummeted as the letter rating scaled up.

4.2.1 Rating Methodologies for Banks

Packer and Tarashev (2011) pointed out that all the three main rating agencies (Fitch Ratings, Moody's Investors Service and Standard and Poor's) noted material worsening in the creditworthiness of European and US banks following the US subprime crisis. They further argued that ramifications to ratings methodologies for banks can represent a double-edged sword for authorities. The reason is based on the fact that policymakers may be subject to credibility issues in the case that ratings contradict official statements. Table 4.1 depicts the rating methodologies for banks adopted by the three major rating agencies. Box 4.1 provides description of the various letters used in credit rating.

Table 4.1 Rating methodologies for banks

	Fitch ratings	*Moody's investors service*	*Standard & poor's*
Stand-alone assessment (intrinsic financial strength)	Focus on off-balance sheet commitments, funding and liquidity risk	Emphasis on forward-looking assessments of capital ratios, based on embedded expected losses	Focus on risk-adjusted performance and ability to grow capital from profits
All-in-rating (with external support)	Distinct ratings of sovereign support provide a floor	Based on a joint default analysis of banks and providers of support	Anticipated support increases with the bank's systemic importance
System-wide assessment Country rating Does systemic risk affect banks' ratings?	Based on: – macro indicators – average bank rating Not explicitly; anticipated support increases with the bank's systemic importance but falls in times of generalized distress	None Not explicitly; anticipated support increases with the bank's systemic importance	Based on: – macro indicators – industry and regulatory environment Yes, through: – macro indicators for countries where the bank operates – assessments of the industry and regulatory environment in the home country
Last major changes	2005: systemic risk analysis	2007: joint default analysis in support assessment	2011: overhaul of the rating methodology Greater emphasis on: – system-wide risks – link from earnings to capital

Source Packer and Tarashev (2011)

Box 4.1: What Do the Letter Ratings Mean?

The general meaning of our credit rating opinions is summarized below.

"AAA"—Extremely strong capacity to meet financial commitments. Highest Rating.

"AA"—Very strong capacity to meet financial commitments.

"A"—Strong capacity to meet financial commitments, but somewhat susceptible to adverse economic conditions and changes in circumstances.

"BBB"—Adequate capacity to meet financial commitments, but more subject to adverse economic conditions.

"BBB−"—Considered lowest investment grade by market participants.

"BB +"—Considered highest speculative grade by market participants.

"BB"—Less vulnerable in the near term but faces major ongoing uncertainties to adverse business, financial and economic conditions.

"B"—More vulnerable to adverse business, financial and economic conditions but currently has the capacity to meet financial commitments.

"CCC"—Currently vulnerable and dependent on favourable business, financial and economic conditions to meet financial commitments.

"CC"—Currently highly vulnerable.

"C"—Currently highly vulnerable obligations and other defined circumstances.

"D"—Payment default on financial commitments.

Note: Ratings from "AA" to "CCC" may be modified by the addition of a plus (+) or minus (−) sign to show relative standing within the major rating categories. *Source: Standard and Poor's website.*

Basel II suggested the need for an internal rating framework to assess the level of capital adequacy. Jayadev (2006) undertook a survey among Indian banks to find that considerable weight (around 40 per cent) is attributed to financial risk under their internal credit rating models. In general, bank's ratings constitute an important ingredient in the sphere of banking and finance.

4.2.2 *Morningstar Corporate Credit Rating Methodology*

Morningstar Corporate Credit Rating (2014) measures the ability of a firm to meet its debt and debt-like commitments. Morningstar Corporate Credit Rating methodology is based on four key components: business risk, cash flow cushion, solvency score and distance to default. The ratings are independent, objective and forward-looking with stress being laid on merging qualitative and quantitative analysis to generate the credit ratings. Maximum scores of 5 are attributed to distinct variables such as management, dependence on capital markets and cyclicality of operations. The distinct credit ratings assigned by Morningstar are depicted in Table 4.2.

ICAP (2013) developed a credit rating methodology to be applied to Greek companies as per the provisions of the Regulation 1060/2009 of the European Parliament and of the Council of 16 September 2009 and CESR's guidelines (10–347) on Credit Rating Agencies. Bond ratings are overwhelmingly perceived as surrogate assessment of the riskiness of bonds. In fact, high-rated bonds sell at substantially lower yields relative to low-rated bonds. Chandy and Duett (1990) argued that liquidity had more weight in rating commercial paper[1] compared to bond rating. Besides, Backer and Gosman (1980) observed that the chief determinant of a commercial paper rating relates to its corresponding bond rating.

4.3 An Overview of European Union and US Institutional Differences

The European Central Bank and the Federal Reserve are widely perceived as major players in the arena of central banking excellence, not only in terms of monetary policy or benchmarking concerns but also in terms of certain important legislations. Indeed, certain important differences prevail between the European Central Bank and the Federal Reserve, as discussed by Cecchetti and O'Sullivan (2003). First, the independence of the European Central Bank is enshrined by its Maastricht Treaty. In spite of the fact that the Federal Reserve also enjoys independence, yet, it must report regularly to the Congress and hence such independence is likely to be affected. Alternatively stated, the Federal Reserve is susceptible to rejoice over less independence than the European Central Bank on the back that the Congress can revoke its delegated responsibility at any point in time. Second, the Federal Reserve is considered to be highly flexible relative to the European Central Bank which has often been obsessed with having low inflation. Third, the Federal Reserve clings to discretion while European Central Bank stick to rules. Fourth,

[1] Commercial paper constitutes a short-term external financing instrument for corporates usually having maturity below nine months.

Table 4.2 Description of credit rating under Morningstar Corporate Credit Rating

Credit rating	*Description*
AAA	**Extremely low default risk**. Issuers rated AAA typically operate wide-moat, low uncertainty businesses and can easily cover all outstanding maturities with cash on hand and one year's worth of free cash flow
AA	**Very low default risk**. Issuers rated AA tend to be wide- or narrow-moat companies with low to medium uncertainty and a Morningstar Cash Flow Cushion that affords a very wide margin of safety against adverse developments
A	**Low default risk**. Issuers rated A typically include wide- or narrow-moat companies with medium to high uncertainty and a Morningstar Cash Flow Cushion that affords a wide margin of safety against adverse developments
BBB	**Moderate default risk**. Issuers rated BBB typically include narrow- or no-moat companies with medium to very high uncertainty and a Morningstar Cash Flow Cushion that affords a modest margin of safety against deteriorating business conditions
BB	**Above-average default risk**. Issuers rated BB typically include no-moat companies with high to very high uncertainty and a Morningstar Cash Flow Cushion that affords a minimal margin of safety against deteriorating business conditions
B	**High default risk**. Issuers rated B typically include no-moat companies with very high uncertainty and a Morningstar Cash Flow Cushion that indicates significant dependence on favourable business conditions
CCC	**Currently very high default risk**. Issuers rated CCC typically include no-moat companies with very high uncertainty and a Morningstar Cash Flow Cushion that indicates significant dependence on favourable business conditions to avoid default or significant capital restructuring
CC	**Currently extreme default risk**. Issuers rated CC typically include no-moat companies with very high or extreme uncertainty and a Morningstar Cash Flow Cushion that indicates extreme dependence on favourable business conditions to avoid default or significant capital restructuring
C	**Imminent payment default**. Morningstar's C rating captures issuers that we believe will encounter default in the very near term, including those firms that have entered into a grace period following a skipped payment of an obligation
D	**In default**. Morningstar reserves a D rating for companies that have defaulted in fact or have declared bankruptcy

Source Morningstar (2014)

Table 4.3 Differences between the ECB and the Federal Reserve

	European Central Bank	*Federal Reserve*
Constituents	National Central Banks	Regional Federal Reserve Banks
Main member	President of ECB chairing the Governing Council meetings	Chairman of the Fed's Board of Governors who chairs the Federal Open Market Committee
Decision-making body	Governing Council; all NCBs governors have an equal vote in decisions	Federal Open Market Committee; voting restrictions are present

the use of interest rates targets, telegraphing the moves of interest rates ahead of policy changes and small interest rate adjustments (termed as gradualism), all contribute towards enhanced transparency of the Federal Reserve. Above all, as stated by Gerdesmeier et al. (2007) the European Central Bank does not publish minutes of its Governing Council meetings compared to the Federal Reserve to avoid political pressures of policy-makers in their home countries. The chief rationale behind gradualism is to shun off destabilizing effects of interest rates that can feasibly peter out the functioning of financial markets. Fifth, in the US, the exchange rate policy is controlled by the Treasury department while in the case of the Eurosystem, the European Central Bank is entitled to formulate the exchange rate policy.

Central bank balances consist of deposits made by private financial institutions. As pointed out by Bowman et al. (2010), the Federal Reserve started to pay interest on both required and excess reserve balances from October 2008. Technically speaking, the floor for market interest rates should be related to the interest rate paid on reserves by central banks. However, unless all institutions which borrow or lend overnight funds are permitted to hold remunerated deposits at the central bank, there will be feasibility for the overnight market rate to trade below the policy rate floor. In stark contrast to the Federal Reserve, the European Central Bank remunerates only required reserves at the average main refinancing rate over the maintenance period while excess reserves (non-reserve deposits) are not remunerated.

In terms of convergence, both European Central Bank and the Federal Reserve agree that money is neutral in the long run, congruous with the classical theory of money. The institutional arrangements tend to be similar as shown in Table 4.3.

4.4 Ratings Methodology

The current section discusses a whole set of metrics employed to derive the ratings for each central bank in the world. A priori, these metrics fall under both qualitative and quantitative components with care being taken to preserve objectivity as far as possible by laying out preset and well-defined ratings criteria. Under certain cases, negative markings are undertaken to deter certain practices as in the following components: negative z-score, incompatibility with international accounting policy, no contact information, failure to adhere to timely reporting, power to control money supply, central bank involvement in debt management task, bank regulation and supervision and governance indicators. To unleash a full-fledged ratings system for central banks, certain widely accepted measures are incorporated via outsourcing from other well-established indices such as governance indicators, central bank independence and banking regulation and supervision. We stick to the approach applied by Thomson Reuters (2013) whereby each indicator is assigned a relative level of significance from 0 to/or 5 in most cases.

(a) **Staff efficiency (0 or 5)**

Staff costs, displayed for each country on the financial statements, constitute the main source for computation of this metric. In essence, the average of the staff costs per personnel, computed over the periods 2000 to 2017/18, is used. Proper exchange rate adjustments are undertaken to ensure that all values are converted into US dollars for ease of comparison. Then, the mean of this value is derived for all the central banks. Subsequently, for all central banks which exhibit values beyond this mean are rated zero while those having values below this threshold are assigned five marks.

The reason for having recourse towards staff efficiency as one of the metrics for central bank ratings is that staff costs represent a major source of costs for central banks worldwide so much so that proper costs control can help in spawning comfortable levels of profits. Such a state of affairs is underscored in light of the crisis which gnawed hard at the earning-generation capacity of central banks in the world. Overall, the staff efficiency measure of assessment is deemed to be particularly vital in gauging on the extent of central bank efficiency in performing their functions.

(b) **Publication of Financial Stability Reports (0, 2 (discontinuity) or 5)**

Central banks worldwide are usually mandated with a price stability function. However, another important function also characterizes central banks in the world; namely that of cushioning the financial system from any undesired shock, susceptible to impair on the stability of the financial system. As a matter of fact, the Borio and Drehman (2009) stated that most central banks work under the assumption that they are endowed with a financial stability role. Moreover, Caruana (2014) argued that central banks play a preponderant role in safeguarding the financial stability of a country chiefly when it comes to ensuring sound implementation of macroprudential surveillance. In addition, Nier (2009) argued that the conventional role of central banks in maintaining price stability, among other roles, should be stretched to contain systemic risks. The publication of financial stability reports undeniably assists in bolstering such macroprudential surveillance process. In that respect, there has been mounting awareness among central banks to disseminate timely and crucial information about the health of their financial system on a regular basis. Most importantly, the crisis unleashed considerable interest in financial stability reports—many countries which previously did not publish financial stability reports, subsequently started to publish them in view of scaling up widespread public interest in financial stability issues. These reports also provided the opportunities for central banks to show their strenuous efforts undertaken to ensure that financial stability risks are kept at the bay without trailing behind detrimental distortions to the whole gamut of their financial system. Five marks are assigned in the case of publication of financial stability reports. No marks are assigned in the case of no publication. In the case of any discontinuity in reporting, only two marks are assigned.

(c) Consumer Price Index (0 or 5)

The European System of Central Banks (ESCB) consists of the European Central Bank and the National Central Banks (NCBs) of the 28 member states of the European Union. The Eurosystem constitutes a subset of the ESCB, i.e. the European Central Bank and all those NCBs which have adopted the euro. The chief objective of the European Central Bank is to main price stability. The monetary policy instruments under the European Central Bank consist of both standard and non-standard measures. The non-standard measures consist of expansion of assets list used as collateral, longer-term liquidity provision and direct purchase of debt securities. The standard measures comprise of three main components, namely, standing facilities (deposit facility and marginal lending facility), open market operations (main refinancing operations, longer-term refinancing operations, fine-tuning operations and structural operations) and reserve requirements (reserve base, reserve ratio and remuneration on reserve holdings). Most importantly, inflation analysis under the European Central Bank is based on two important components: economic analysis and monetary analysis.

The main aim of the Federal Reserve is to maintain price stability, maximum employment and moderate long-term interest rates. The Federal Reserve employs the following tools as instruments for monetary policy implementation: open market operations, discount window (based on borrowings by monetary financial institutions on a short-term basis) and reserve requirements.

The composition of the central bank rating approach would have been incomplete without catering for the ability to maintain low inflation values which are conductive to growth. As a matter of fact, many economists widely agree that low inflation assists in greasing the sands of the economic wheels to thereby stimulate higher levels of growth. Based on the crucial function of price stability maintenance, marks are allocated to central banks which exhibit inflation rates below the mean inflation rate value for all central banks. This is effected after computing the average inflation rate for the period 2000 to 2017/18 for all the central banks. Five marks are assigned to central banks which display inflation values below the mean value and zero marks for the reverse scenario.

(d) **Language use on the website for dissemination of information (0 or 5)**

The Bank for International Settlements (2009) stated that "better communication about central bank actions is essential in reducing the uncertainty facing economic agents". Most importantly, during periods of liquidity trap where interest rates hover near zero bounds, effective central bank communication is key to shape future expectations, as underscored by Bernanke et al. (2004). The quality of communication conveyed is thus directly tributary on the type of language used. In most countries of the world, English does not happen to be the main language to the plain effect that the use of a common language on the central bank website constitutes the best medium to enhance the flow of communication to the public. Subsequently, five marks are attributed to central banks which resort to more than one language for the dissemination of information to outsiders. The underlying rationale is that at least two languages used on the website glaringly demonstrate the committed efforts of the central banks to be close to the public in terms of closer understanding of their policies. The latter helps to leverage the credibility of central banks which latter helps to consolidate price stability via proper anchoring of inflation expectations. Above all, ensuring the display of information in at least one international language such as English or French helps to improve information flow to foreigners. In exceptional cases where English is the medium for spoken language, the use of one language is positively marked, namely in the case of the US, UK, Australia, Bermuda and Cayman Islands.

(e) **Research papers (0 or 5)**

Research is of paramount significance for any central bank in the world as it unleashes the best policies to be taken to obviate any backfiring effects of originally contemplated policies. In the words of Shirakawa (2013) "Good decision making and research supporting a central bank are the real foundation of its independence." For instance, in his opening message in the Bank of Canada 2010 Annual Report, Mark Carney, the governor of the Bank of Canada, pointed out that research and policy analysis constituted one of the key priorities at the central bank in light of the financial crisis to shape out better policies. In a parallel manner,

Cecchetti (2002), in a Study Center Gerzensee Newsletter, stated the following opening remarks: "Every central bank should strive to produce high-quality research; that is, written products of general interest to the people outside of the central bank. As an institution entrusted with improving a country's economic well-being, the central bank is a natural place to produce contributions to knowledge". Similarly, the Bank for International Settlements has an online central bank research hub.[2]

No central bank can operate without a lubrifying monetary policy transmission model. In that respect, constant research in monetary policy is regarded as a commendable feature of any central bank in the world. However, research should not only be confined to the realm of monetary policy but should also stretch to core areas such as stress testing, financial literacy, modelling of real estate bubbles, among others. To sieve out the intensity of research undertaken, the total number of research papers displayed on the websites of central banks is used with papers written in English language only being considered since locally used language in research papers fails to be useful to the general global audience. The laid out benchmark relates to the mean value of the number of research papers. Five marks are allocated to a central bank in the case that it is endowed with above mean number of research papers.

(f) **Z-Score (Negative markings in case of negative z-score values; 0, 5 or −10)**

The composition of global central bank ratings would not have been full-fledged if no due consideration were to be given to the robustness of central banks' profitability and equity. To gauge on the strength of central banks, recourse is made towards z-score values which are computed as net profits (before exceptional items and foreign exchange gains/losses) over total assets, added with equity over total assets, all of which are then divided by the standard deviation of net profits over total assets. As a matter of fact, the Altman z-score pertains to non-financial firms when gauging their probability of default. Fortunately, there is a z-score which applies specifically to financial firms as developed by Hannan and

[2] Link: http://www.bis.org/cbhub/.

Hanweck (1988) and applied by Bertay et al. (2013), among others. Hannan and Hanweck (1988) developed the z-score to have an estimate of the perceived probability of insolvency for banks where insolvency is defined as a state when present losses exhaust capital. Technically speaking, the z-score captures the number of times returns on assets can decline before a central bank is subject to distressful conditions (usually captured via negative equity) and is defined as follows:

$$\text{Z-score} = \frac{\text{ROA} + \text{Capital to asset ratio}}{\text{Standard deviation of ROA}}$$

where ROA pertains to returns on assets and capital to asset ratio is captured by equity to total assets.

The quality of profitability generated is particularly important in enshrining the equity position, thereby explaining the use of profitability and equity in the composition of the z-score. Robust central banks are anticipated to depict stronger z-score values. The threshold value is captured via the mean value. Central banks which are endowed with above average z-score mean values are assigned five marks as it shows lower probability of going into distress, i.e. being subject to negative equity. Conversely, central banks which demonstrate below mean values score zero marks. In extreme cases where central banks report negative z-score values, minus ten marks are allocated. The underlying rationale is that negative equity values are synonymous to poor credibility and transparency in the implementation of monetary policy.

(g) **Risk management information for at least 3 years (0 or 5)**

Risk management constitutes an integral part of any institution, whether financial or non-financial. As a matter of fact, the Organisation for Economic Cooperation and Development (2014) reviewed the risk management practices of 27 jurisdictions to then-state that "The process of risk management and the results of risk assessments should be appropriately disclosed". In a parallel manner, the Basel Committee on Banking Supervision (2013) came out with a set of principles to consolidate banks' risk data aggregation and capabilities and internal risk reporting practices. The Basel Committee on Banking Supervision further stated that accurate, complete and timely data constitutes a core element for effective risk management, let alone the presentation of the right information to the right people at the right time to ensure effective risk management.

The ultimate aim of providing information on risk management is geared towards assessing the potential implications of risks on the bottom line and future survival of an institution. Above all, by showing the risks and actions taken to mitigate them, distinct institutions tend to embellish their image as risk considerate business performers which can feasibly boost up their market values. The empirical literature on risk management is rife with evidence of sound risk management trailing behind rising market values of firms following the work of Allayannis and Weston (2001), who were the first to demonstrate that hedging directly impacted on firm value with a 5 per cent difference in market value on average in the case of foreign currency derivatives users compared to non-users. Five marks are allocated in the case that a central bank reports information on risk management for at least three years. The usual risks under focus comprises of credit risk, liquidity risk, currency risk and interest rate risk. Credit risks are usually captured in dual form; a geographical decomposition part and a net asset exposure while currency risks are taken as net exchange rate exposure under major currencies such as US dollars, Euros, and British pound, among others. No marks are given in the case of no risks reporting or risk reporting of less than 3 years.

(h) **International Accounting Policy used (Negative marks if no compatibility; 0 or −5)**

The US Generally Accepted Accounting Principles (GAAP) or International Financial Reporting Standards (IFRS) constitutes the two widely used accounting frameworks in the world. Subsequently, each annual report is checked to ensure that either of these two frameworks has been implemented. Moreover, due consideration is also given to European Central Bank guidelines for European countries. Should this be the case, then zero marks are assigned, otherwise negative five marks are allocated to the central bank. The main gist of such a metric is to ensure the highest level of integrity, transparency and accountability when it comes to reporting of financial statements. Ironically, based on their strategic role that they play in any economy, it is of paramount significance to ensure that central bank financials are prepared in line with the highest level of fairness, transparency and integrity. Otherwise, the validity of the reported statements becomes questionable.

(i) **Quality of the Website (0 to 10)**

Central banks are not different from database warehouses as they produce significant amount of critical economic data widely used for research not only by themselves but also by academics. Sound, comprehensive, timely and sophisticated data retrieval systems become a sine qua non condition for an effectively functioning central bank. Apart from the data retrieval system, the home page of each central bank is assessed in terms of quality information disseminated such as presentation quality of information-how different themes (History, Monetary Policy, Payments and Settlement systems, etc.) are presented and accessed on the website. The ease of accessibility options has also been considered, let alone any distinctive features which substantially enhance the home page. Furthermore, the level of information coverage is also given due consideration. Overall, 10 marks are assigned to quality of the website and each central bank is rated accordingly. Strict adherence to the selected criteria is made to ensure that objectivity in rating is preserved under quality of the website.

(j) **Adherence to Green concept (0 or 5)**

Climate change is now deemed as a burning issue for any country in the world as it calls forth vigorous ramifications at all levels of the production–consumption processes to undermine the level of carbon footprint. The world is thereby steadily being engulfed with innovative green financial products such as green car loans, energy efficiency mortgages, alternative energy venture capital, eco-savings deposits, and "green" credit cards to reconcile the financial needs with environmental concerns, as widely commented in United Nations Environment Programme Finance Initiative (2007). Tietenberg (1998) pointed out that public disclosure of the environmental performance of companies has been featured as the third wave of environmental regulation, post the command-and-control and market-based approaches. Most importantly, the World Bank (2014) published data on various environmental-linked metrics for many countries of the world under its little green data book. However, the metrics pertained mainly to broader environmental activities such as water and sanitation, energy and emissions, and oceans, among others. No consideration is given to the level of green attainment in central banking activities.

Proactive and considerate central banks are expected to cling towards greener activities in view of pushing forward the concept of a green economy at all sphere of their activities. Five marks are assigned in the case that a central bank demonstrates evidence of green concept implementation in its activities such as efficient consumption of electricity, own electricity generation, investment in greener materials during extension of buildings, investments in green products, among others.

The annual reports are thoroughly scrutinized to sieve out any commitment towards greener activities. In essence, the reports are scanned for the words "green" to identify strong commitments towards eco-friendly activities.

(k) **Contact information (0 or −5)**

One of the major facets of a good institution relates to its ability to effectively communicate with outsiders. This requires an effective contact detail which is usually in the form of an email address. Based on the heightened level of responsibility assigned to central banks, posting of a contact medium on their websites is deemed a normal feature of their operational activities. No marks are thereby assigned in the case that central banks provide a medium for communication. Otherwise, minus five marks are assigned in the case of absence of any effective contact details. In the case of availability of only telephone numbers, negative marks are assigned because communication via telephone constitutes a costly medium of communication compared to emails. The negative marking is undertaken to cater for the absence of any communication medium and thereby reflects the lack of mutual interaction between a central bank and the outsiders. Most importantly, under the current technological era, it is ironical that a central bank is not equipped with a proper and costless contact channel. The metric used is clear and not opaque as it is the case of a study performed by Demertzis and Hallett (2007). They constructed a model to gauge on the impact of central bank transparency on inflation and output gap for nine OECD countries. Their findings showed that increases in the extent of transparency did not impact on the average levels of inflation and output. They attributed these results as to their transparency index capturing some other elements of central bank actions.

(l) **IMF above mean age maturity (5 or 0 marks)**

Customer banking relationship constitutes an important channel for securing better and higher quality banking services such as finer interest rates or lower charge for commissions and fees. In a parallel manner, closer bonds established for longer periods of time with international institutions help to shape better quality services which eventually trail behind enhanced levels of activities. Indeed, Miwa and Ramseyer (2005) found that large Japanese firms had long-term relationship with one main bank. Such relationship banking is vital but can be downplayed by crisis conditions. For example, Hale (2011) built a global banking network of 7938 banking institutions from 141 countries to assess the formation of new relationships between banks during 1980–2009 time period. Hale found that recessions and banking crises unleashed detrimental impacts on new relationships formations.

Viewed from this perspective, countries which have been members of IMF for a longer time period, are expected to avail of better services, whether from loans side or from technical assistance. Under loans channel, countries which exhibit commitments towards loans and ensure that the funds are used as per cited infrastructural projects, are susceptible to avail of more future loans with respect to additional infrastructural investments to be undertaken. Under technical assistance, countries which have been working with IMF for longer time periods tend to avail of greater knowledge and expertise in macroeconomic modelling and country risk management to consolidate on their financial stability level. Central banks also benefit in terms of enshrined knowledge in modelling their monetary policy transmission mechanism as to ensure the full potency of their decisions. Beyond that, by joining IMF earlier, a country showed its commitment towards higher level of international cooperation. Five marks are allocated to central banks which exhibit above mean age with IMF with zero marks given in the case that such a threshold is not breached.

(m) **Notes to financial statements (5 or 0 marks)**

Presentations of income statements, cash flow statements and balance sheets, are all key ingredients of financial reporting. However, notes to financial statements constitute the most important medium of information dissemination in view of leveraging on the quality of understanding, let alone providing more refined information on financials. As a matter of fact, the European Financial Reporting Advisory Group (2012) stipulated that "The disclosures in the notes should provide information which amplifies and explains the primary financial statements". Above all, notes to financial statements are so vital that, without them, it becomes difficult to gain insight on the financials. For instance, an item like operating expenses on the income statement does not convey much meaning if it is not split into its various components such as staff costs and depreciation, among others. In the same vein, financial statements do not provide explicit information on the risk management activities such as net currency exposure, net interest rate gap and net liquidity gap. This information is usually captured in the lower part of the notes to the financial statements. No marks are given in the case of absence or insufficient notes to the financial statements.

(n) **Conferences/Workshops/Seminars (2 or 0 marks)**

The Bank for International Settlements and the Basel Committee on Banking Supervision jointly created the Financial Stability Institute (FSI) in 1999 to help supervisors worldwide to enshrine their financial systems through FSI's activities which encompass conferences, workshops, seminars and fellowship programmes. In the same vein, as part of their committed tasks to strengthen their technical expertise and boost knowledge, central banks regularly organize workshops, conferences and seminars. The latter are usually posted on the websites of central banks. These events are preponderant as they set the pace for eventually high-quality research in needy areas. For instance, post the onset of the crisis, there has been an increase in research in the area of central banking and financial stability. Moreover, these events bolster the relationships of central bankers at the international level which eventually help to shape better policies in reinforcing bank supervision such as banking resolution. Should a central bank demonstrate evidence of any of these three events on its website, two marks are assigned to it, otherwise no marks are given.

(o) **IMF member (0 or 5 marks)**

Conceived in 1944 but born in 1946, the International Monetary Fund is now a respected multilateral organization that consists of 188 countries worldwide and serves six major roles as discussed by Weiss (2014): fostering international monetary cooperation, enlarging the balanced growth of international trade, promoting exchange rate stability, removing barriers to international capital flows, maintaining confidence by making funds available to member countries and adjusting the balance of payments imbalances in an orderly manner. Nearly all countries in the world are members of the IMF. Such a membership confers important benefits such as country risk assessments on a regular basis (usually on a cycle of 12 months), both technical and financial assistance and critical advice furnished during difficult times. Beyond that, during periods of extreme stress levels, IMF provides special assistance to its members as glaringly shown by the Special Drawing Rights unleashed to relieve countries of detrimental effects of the recent crisis. In that respect, five marks are assigned to all countries which are members of the IMF. No marks are given in the case of non-member countries. The underlying rationale for such a metric is that non-members of IMF are susceptible to avail of lesser coordination and lesser assistance at the international level by virtue of being symptomatic to lower involvements with international authorities. In addition, a non-member of IMF can signify a lesser open and transparent approach to central bank activities.

(p) **Timely reporting (0 or −5)**

Timely reporting of financial information is critical to ensure prompt availability of information for onwards proactive actions. When it comes to central banks annual reports, it is imperative that not only the reporting cycle is preserved but also the issuance of the reports manifest on a timely basis for diverse reasons. First, timely reporting ensures that there has been no tampering of information and that fairness, transparency and accountability have been maintained at all levels of reporting. In fact, the International Monetary Fund (1999) defined transparency as "an environment in which the objectives of policy, its legal, institutional, and economic framework, policy decisions and their rationale, data and information related to monetary and financial policies, and the terms of agencies' accountability, are provided to the public on an understandable, accessible and timely basis". Second, timely reporting enables to have the right information at the right time to enable correct actions to be initiated in view of tackling any upcoming risks or difficulties. For instance, if there are signs of undermined equity which can jeopardize the credibility of the central bank, the reporting of weak equity would enable the government to know that there is a need to keep aside some funds to replenish the equity base of the central bank-quasi-fiscal costs implications of poor central bank equity. Negative marks of five are assigned in case of any infringement on timely reporting, exceeding two years. One year buffer period is allowed meaning that the reporting date of an annual report at time t can be extended to $t + 1$ but not $t + 2$. This buffer time period is to cater for some unforeseen contingencies which may buffet timely reporting but it is unlikely that unexpected events creep in for more than two years.

(q) **Professional Accounting Firms (0 or 5)**

The quality of financial statements hinges a lot on the quality of the accounting firm hired. At the global level, the widely used accounting firms are KPMG, Ernst & Young, Deloitte & Touche, Pricewaterhousecoopers and Grant Thornton. For instance, The International Federation of Accountants (2005) set forth the code of ethics for professional accountants such as integrity, objectivity, professional competence and due care, confidentiality and professional behaviour. In the case that a central bank has its financial statements prepared by any of the five accounting firms, then, they positively marked as they cling to excellence in reporting. Should the reverse manifests, then, nil marks are allocated to the central bank. The ultimate aim of such a metric is to ascertain that the quality of information is maintained at the highest level possible to thereby shun off any potential manipulations.

(r) **Stress Testing (0 or 5 marks)**

Stress testing exercises are perceived as vital tools when it comes to gauging on the vulnerability of institutions to extreme but plausible events. In essence, stress tests are conducted to distil down any major risks susceptible to impact on the health of the local financial system as to gnaw at the financial stability level at the country level. IMF staff conduct stress testing under its macroprudential purposes, notably under Financial Sector Assessment Programs (IMF/World Bank, 2003). Indeed, Jobst et al. (2013) focussed on the solvency stress testing framework applied in the IMF's surveillance of member countries to generate useful guidance for country authorities to prepare their Financial Sector Assessment Programs. The Basel Committee on Banking Supervision (2009) published a document entitled "Principles for sound stress testing practices and supervision" whereby best practices were laid not only for banks but also for central banks. For the latter, the Basel Committee on Banking Supervision (2009) pointed out that "Supervisors should make regular and comprehensive assessments of a bank's stress testing programme". Hence, central banks should be vigorously involved in stress testing exercises.

Alternatively stated, central banks play a critical role in the implementation of sound stress testing exercises as they usually act as supervisors in safeguarding the financial stability level of their countries. By wielding stress testing tools, central banks are best able to undertake timely identification of risks and initiate corresponding measures to obviate any financial system crash. Central banks which regularly undertake stress testing exercises are assigned five marks. Annual reports and websites of the central banks are searched and examined to see if they contain the words of "stress tests".

(s) **Debt Management (0 or −5)**

The Committee on the Global Financial System (2011) discussed the interactions of sovereign debt management with monetary conditions and financial stability with stress being laid on close communication among the relevant agencies such as central banks and debt management units but with each agency maintaining its independence and accountability for its respective role. Such an approach is compatible with Principle 6 from the Stockholm Principles: Guiding principles for managing sovereign risk and high levels of public debt,[3] which were endorsed by debt managers and central bankers from both advanced and emerging market economies.

Conflicts of objectives prevail between debt managers and central bankers. Debt managers attempt to scale down the borrowing costs and thereby prefer a steepening yield curve having low costs structure at the shorter maturity spectrum. However, central bankers tend to distort the redemption profile of debt structures by issuing higher levels of short-term instruments at the expense of experiencing costly issuance of longer-term instruments. The major lesson learnt is that the presence of a debt management function inside a central bank is susceptible to categorically compromise on the effectiveness of monetary policy implementation. As a matter of fact, one of the preset conditions for an effective monetary policy strategy relates to its independence from debt management activities. For instance, Filardo et al. (2012) focussed on the impact of the maturity structure of government debt on yield curve and subsequently on monetary policy in the case of emerging market economies. They further argued that such ramifications in the yield curve can engender repercussions on banking sector lending.

The best avenue to ensure such monetary policy independence is to put in place robust demarcation line whereby debt management activities do not fall under the purview of central banking activities or debt management activities are not undertaken in the premises of the central banks. Otherwise, significant conflict of interests and manipulations are likely to hold so that monetary policy can be manipulated to reduce the public debt costs to the benefit of the government but at the expense of proper economic management of the economy. The ratings structure adopted, should give due consideration to the debt management function. Negative five marks are assigned to central banks which are involved in debt management activities; otherwise, no marks are assigned.

(t) **Inflation targeting[4] (0 or 5 marks)**

Inflation targeting constitutes the highest level of task fulfilment of a central bank in best anchoring inflation expectations. In a speech

[3] Online link: http://www.imf.org/external/np/mcm/Stockholm/principles.htm.

[4] The reference guide is http://www.centralbanknews.info/p/inflation-targets.html for central banks adhering to inflation targeting, updated list as at 2014.

delivered by Mervyn King (2012), the latter pointed out that inflation targeting along with central bank independence contributed significantly in bringing price stability in the UK. Mishkin (2000) set forth a five-pronged definition of inflation targeting which consists of public announcement of the medium-term inflation targets, a commitment by the central bank to price stability, use of a set of variables (monetary, exchange rates and others) to decide on the policy instruments setting, enhanced transparency of monetary policy via communication to the public and bolstered accountability of the central bank to meet its inflation targets.

The first country in the world to ever adhere to inflation targeting was New Zealand post of which many other countries follow suit. Technically speaking, inflation targeting imposes stringent rules when it comes to gauging on changes in interest rate decisions so that biasedness is kept at bay. Apart from spurring objectivity, inflation targeting also contributes towards a smooth flow of information as to stimulate an enhanced level of communication to the general public—a plus point with respect to credibility of monetary policy.

The chief advent of inflation targeting pertains to its requirement for an objective and sophisticated modelling framework which helps in smothering or muting down subjective analyses. Nonetheless, the benefits of adhering to inflation targeting are widely debated. McDermott (2012) pointed out that inflation targeting was highly helpful for the Reserve Bank of New Zealand as it helped to induce credibility during the global financial crisis. Mishkin (2000) argued that inflation targeting does not constitute a panacea so that it may not be apt for many emerging economies.

In practice, there are two types of inflation targeting in the world-explicit and implicit. Explicit inflation targeting central banks clearly stipulate a range within which inflation should hover around. Implicit inflation targeting central banks constitute those central banks which stick towards stated inflation targeting preset by their monetary union. Subsequently, all euro area members are positively rated based on their inherent objective of clinging to the Maastricht Treaty.

(u) **Power to control money supply (−5 to 0)**

Monetary policy is overwhelmingly deemed as one of the core underpinnings to ensure the smooth functioning of an economy. Countries found under the euro zone area are constrained in their ability to influence the level of money supply based on the use of a single common currency. The Bank for International Settlements (2009) clearly pointed out that "... national central banks make no independent monetary policy decisions as institutions". During periods of stress, these countries are not able to properly influence the level of money supply to spawn the desired level of local economic activities. In a parallel manner, countries which adhere to fixed exchange rate regimes are endowed with limited power in influencing their levels of money supply. Under currency boards, there are similar impotencies in fine-tuning monetary policy to shun away detrimental shocks. To establish a sound and consistent demarcation line, countries exhibiting floating or managed float exchange rate regimes are not negatively marked.

(v) **Central bank independence (0 to 5)**

Many studies have been undertaken in the sphere of central bank independence. The pioneering research in the area of monetary policy and political intervention relates to the works of Kydland and Prescott (1977) and Barro and Gordon (1983) who studied how time-inconsistency problems and political pressures distorted the monetary authority's incentives under various institutional arrangements. Rogoff (1985) further proposed to delegate the tasks of monetary policy to an independent central bank. Siklos (2008) argued that there is no single definition for central bank independence which applies to all countries. Inquisitive readers may refer to Jakob de Haan et al. (2008) for a background version of literature pertaining to central bank independence. Alpanda and Honig (2009) did not find evidence of monetary policy manipulations during elections in case of independent central banks for both advanced and developing countries.

Chrigui et al. (2011) assessed the legal and real independence of the Tunisian Central Bank to find a positive and insignificant correlation between real independence and inflation. Jacome and Vazquez (2008) showed evidence of an inverse relationship between central bank independence and inflation in the case of 24 Latin American and Caribbean countries. Recently, Ueda and Valencia (2012) focussed on macroprudential regulation and monetary policy interactions. Their findings showed that a non-independent macroprudential regulator operating with an independent monetary authority posted improved results relative to a non-independent central bank, bestowed with the dual functions of price and financial stability. Similarly, Weymark (2007) showed that partial central bank independence can be optimal. Hefeker and Zimmer (2011) concluded that full central bank independence is not optimal in the case of uncertain central bank preferences. Förch and Sunde (2012) found evidence of economic independence of central bank being more important than political independence when it comes to assessing central bank independence's impact on stock market returns in the case of emerging countries.

To date, different versions of central bank independence were built. Grilli et al. (1991) constructed a central bank independence index that integrated the dual components of political independence and economic independence. They defined political independence as the ability to choose policy objectives independently, freed from any governmental involvement. Political independence is captured by metrics such as whether or not the government appoints the governor and the board, whether government representatives sit on the board and whether government approval is needed for monetary policy. Economic independence is defined as the ability to wield instruments of monetary policy without limitations such as the extent to which a central bank is needed to finance government deficit. Cukierman et al. (1992) developed a criteria to capture central bank independence as follows: the governor is appointed by the board of the central bank in lieu of the prime minister or the minister of finance with a long-term appointment in office, policy decisions are taken without government involvement, main stated objective of the central bank is price stability and limits are being imposed on the ability of the government to borrow from the central bank. Cukierman et al. (1992) combined these four components to generate an index of central bank independence.

The literature on central bank independence heavily hinges on central bank governor turnover, yet, such a variable is not freed from major shortcomings. For instance, the turnover of central bank governors is likely to be dominated by political motives in lieu of pure financial needs. For instance, Alesina and Summers (1993) investigated the link between central bank independence and variability of economic growth. They found that monetary discipline scaled down inflation variability but did not entail considerable benefits in terms of real macroeconomic performance. They further commented that "... the degree of central bank independence is only one of several institutional factors, exchange rate arrangements, and exogenous shocks that influence economic performance in different countries". Third, some studies showed that central bank independence is of a much larger dimension. For instance, Hielscher and Markwardt (2012) found evidence that higher autonomy given to a central bank did not necessarily trail behind better inflation performance in the case of a sample of 69 countries. They argued that two conditions must be met, namely a large change in independence and a high quality of political institutions. In a parallel manner, Hayat and Farvaque (2012) came up with the evidence that inflation performance was not enough to account for people's preference for an independent central bank. They found that other features such as gender, employment status, education level, income quartiles, extent of information and civic issues are being particularly important.

Dreher et al. (2007) argued that the central bank governor turnover rate is linked to political instability, elections and past inflation. Cukierman (1992) pointed out that the turnover rate seemed to be an acceptable independence proxy for the developing countries. Dreher et al. (2010) worked out a database containing the turnover of central bank governors worldwide based on legal duration in office and time in office.

Dincer and Eichengreen (2014) found that central bank independence has increased over time for many countries in the world. Dincer and Eichengreen (2014) augmented the Cukierman et al. (1992) measure of central bank independence by incorporating elements such as restrictions on the reappointment of the CEO, provisions impacting on (re)appointment of other board members, limits on government representation on the board and intervention of the government in exchange rate policy formulation to thereby generate a highly comprehensive measure of central bank independence, labelled as Central Bank Independence Weighted (CBIW) which is used in the current rating methodology. In the case a country is not present, its index value is assumed to be zero. The minimum and maximum values of the index values are used for conversion purposes so that the assigned scores range from zero to five marks as follows.

$$\text{Marks scored} = \frac{\text{i Index Value} - \text{Minimum Index Value}}{\text{Maximum Index Value} - \text{Minimum Index Value}} \times 5$$

(w) **Bank regulation and supervision in the world**

Bank regulation and supervision has been subject to immense scrutiny in light of the crisis. Proposed by former US Federal Reserve chairman Paul Volcker and implemented as part of the Dodd-Frank legislation, the Volcker rule was approved by US regulators in December 2013. The main objective of the Volcker Rule is to restrict US banks from investing into speculative investments. The rule applies to both domestic and foreign banks, let alone to any participant in a securities or derivatives transaction that resides in the US. The European Commission also proposed a version of the Volcker Rule for European banks in order to obviate the "too-big-to-fail" banking risks, as experienced during the fallout of the US subprime crisis in 2007/08. The aim is to put a ban on proprietary trading.

As per the European Union Bank Recovery and Resolution Directive (BRRD), the word "Resolution" signifies the restructuring of a bank to ensure the continuity of its operations while simultaneously preserving financial stability and putting critical components into insolvency proceedings. Another critical role played by bank resolution relates to mitigation of moral hazard problems by ensuring that bank failures are not being funded via taxpayers' money but instead by the capital of equity holders and debtholders. In 2010, the US set up a resolution framework for systemic financial institutions under the Dodd-Frank Act whereby the Federal Deposit Insurance Corporation takes any bruised bank into receivership to then either transform it into a new entity or close down with losses being shared between shareholders and creditors, respectively.

Čihák et al. (2012) examined the World Bank's 2011–2012 Bank Regulation and Supervision Survey. They found considerable differences between crisis and non-crisis countries in various aspects of regulation and supervision such as less stringent definitions of capital, restrictions on non-bank activities, treatment quality of bad loans and loan losses and incentives for private sector to monitor banks' risks. Barth et al. (2013) also undertook intensive surveys with respect to bank regulation and supervision for 180 countries in the world with focus being also laid on changes in banking policies over time. The current rating methodology incorporates three components developed by Barth et al. (2013) to capture the dynamics of the quality of bank regulation and supervision over time worldwide. The three components are as follows: change in the index of bank capital regulations, change in the index of official supervisory power and change in the index of deposit insurance, all based on Survey I to IV.

Barth et al. (2013) built an index of deposit insurer power to capture the level of a country's deposit insurance regime which is also being tracked since 1999–2011. The constituents of the deposit insurance index are made of various questions such as the legal power of the deposit insurance authority, ability of the deposit insurance fund to take actions in the case of violations, ability of the regulatory body to seize the holding company or the subsidiary company, among others. They also built an index of official supervisory power to capture the extent to which an economy's bank supervisory agency has the vested power to take actions as and when required. To serve that purpose, a plethora of questions are used such as power of the supervisory agency to meet external auditors, vested power of the regulatory body to alter the organizational structure of a bank and to supersede shareholders' rights, among others. Finally, Barth et al. (2013) constructed an index for bank capital regulators to reflect the level of capital that banks must hold. They used a series of questions pertaining to minimum capital-asset ratio, foreign exchange losses and sources of funds eligible to be used as capital, among others.

The index values found for the metric change in the index of deposit insurance from survey I to IV were considered as direct score values, ranging from −3 (less power) to 3 (more power). The index values found for the metric change in the index of bank capital regulations from survey I to IV were considered as direct score values, ranging from −5 (less stringent) to 6 (more stringent). The index values found for the metrics change in the index of official supervisory powers from survey I to IV were considered as direct score values, ranging from −7.50 (less power/less stringent) to 9 (more power/more stringent), which were then halved to generate marks in the range of −3.75 to 4.5 marks. In the case that a country is not found in the given metric under consideration, zero marks are assigned. The values were extracted from Figs. 9, 10 and 13 found in the paper of Barth et al. (2013).

(x) **Global Regulatory Framework for banks under Basel III (0, 2.5 or 5)**

Basel II gave due consideration to credit, market and operational risks. However, the US Subprime crisis glaringly showed the limitations of Basel II in terms of its inability to effectively factor in liquidity risk, mostly felt via frozen interbank markets for the banking sector. The Basel Committee on Banking Supervision reforms introduced Basel III to consolidate the level of liquidity risk in the global banking framework. Four important features are embodied in the Basel III framework in terms of liquidity coverage ratio, net stable funding ratio, principles for sound liquidity risk management and supervisory monitoring. The liquidity coverage ratio stipulates banks to maintain ample high-quality liquid assets to bear a 30-day stressed funding scenario which is specified by supervisors. Under the net stable funding ratio, the aim is to deal with liquidity mismatches at longer-term levels to ensure that banks cling stable sources of funding. Under the guidance of principles for sound liquidity risk management, the objective is based on taking aboard lessons learnt from the crisis in view of reviewing the sound practices for managing liquidity risk in banks. Under supervisory monitory, monitoring metrics are applied to help supervisors in their supervisory tasks in terms of liquidity risk assessment at both individual banks level and system-wide level.

The Bank for International Settlements published information with respect to the progress report on the implementation of the Basel regulatory framework concerning the status of adoption of Basel III at end of March 2013. Three distinct colours are used to capture the status of Basel III adoption. Green signifies that the Basel III regulatory framework adoption has already been completed so that all countries found in this category are assigned five marks. Yellow means that the Basel III regulatory framework is still in process and hence countries falling into this category are assigned 2.5 marks. Red implies that there is no progress with respect to this regulatory framework so that nil marks are assigned. All countries not found in the coloured cells are accordingly assigned zero marks.

(y) **Worldwide Governance Indicators (0 or 5)**
(i) **The Corporate Library, Institutional Shareholder Services Inc. and GovernanceMetrics International**

The Organisation for Economic Cooperation and Development[5] defines corporate governance as follows: "Corporate Governance looks at the institutional and policy framework for corporations—from their very beginnings, in entrepreneurship, through their governance structures, company law, privatisation, to market exit and insolvency. The integrity of corporations, financial institutions and markets is particularly central to the health of our economies and their stability". The Corporate Library datasets generate yearly corporate governance datasets from the year 2001 to 2013. A large set of above 3000 US companies are involved with main data categories consisting of the following metrics: Corporate Board Structure and Independence, Director Positions and Committee Assignments, Executive Compensation, Director Compensation, Audit Fees, Takeover Defenses and Corporate Ownership.

The Institutional Shareholder Services Inc. constitutes another world's leading provider of corporate governance solutions but for distinct types of clients such as asset owners, hedge funds and asset service providers. The Institutional Shareholder Services's solutions incorporate objective governance research and recommendations, end-to-end proxy voting and distribution solutions, among others. The Institutional Shareholder Services Inc. was sold in 2007 to RiskMetrics. GovernanceMetrics International is another company which plays a critical role in US public markets. The main benefit of these corporate governance ratings is that they help investors to shun off bad investments. Indeed, the Institutional Shareholder Services Inc. pointed out that its ratings helped investment managers to avoid massive losses during the meltdown at Enron, Global Crossing and WorldCom. GovernanceMetrics International focusses on the premise that the use of corporate governance ratings assist firms in generating superior returns over time. These three rating institutions differ in terms of focus, approach and sample coverage but convergence in terms of evaluation of a large sample of public firms in the US.

The Institutional Shareholder Services Inc. ratings focus on data gleaned from public filings and company surveys conducted under eight

[5] OECD website.

specific categories: board of directors (composition, independence), audit, charter and bylaw provisions, anti-takeover provisions, executive and director compensation, progressive practices (such as performance reviews and succession plans), ownership and director education. The Institutional Shareholder Services Inc. implement more than 4000 statistical tests based on 16 measures of risk and performance to end up with the optimal weighting of 64 governance variables in its Corporate Governance Quotient, as its main corporate governance rating. GovernanceMetrics International collects data on several hundred governance mechanisms such as compensation, takeover defense, board mechanism, firm's compliance with securities regulations, stock exchange listing requirements, among others. A scoring algorithm is applied which weigh each metric as per investor's interest to then compute a rating from 1 to 10. The algorithm penalises outliers and ranks each firm relative to other firms for a large sample of more than 4000 companies. Compared to proprietary quantitative data analysis undertaken by Institutional Shareholder Services Inc. and GovernanceMetrics International, The Corporate Library factors in subjective judgement and expertise with respect to a company's governance quality. In essence, The Corporate Library focusses on four important areas, namely, company's board and succession planning, CEO practices, takeover defenses and board-level concerns. Each company is then assigned a grade from A to F.

(ii) **Thomson Reuters Corporate Responsibility Ratings**

Thomson Reuters (2013) developed ratings for corporate and social responsibility for 4600 public firms globally based on ASSET4, a Thomson Reuters business which unleashes environmental, social and governance information based on 250+ key performance indicators. Broad pillars are embedded in the data aggregations as depicted in Table 4.4. Thomson Reuters (2013) adopted certain standards with respect to the ratings such as all data being quantitative, no definitive approach used to weigh the key performance indicators and less weight being given to key performance indicators which repeated the same information and also to Boolean type variables. In addition, certain considerations were observed when determining the weights such as relevance, independent information and objective measurability. Furthermore, in the case of the

Table 4.4 Components of pillars under Thomson Reuters

Pillars	*Components*
Environmental pillar	Emission reduction, Product innovation, Resource reduction
Governance pillar	Board functions, Board structure, Compensation policy, Shareholders policy, Vision-and-strategy
Social pillar	Community, diversity, employment quality, health and safety, human rights, product responsibility, training and development

social weightings, each key performance indicator was assigned a relative level of significance which ranges from 0 to 5.

(iii) **Applied Governance Indices**

It is widely recognized that corporate governance quality plays a critical role in the quality of central banks in the world. The underlying rationale is based on the interactions which subsist among distinct economic players, including the private and the public sectors. However, the empirical work got a real momentum in light of the work performed by La Porta et al. (1997, 1998) who analysed the economic impacts of corporate governance regulation. Grossman and Hart (1980) and Shleifer and Vishny (1986) argued for the prevalence of executive compensation contracts to mitigate the conflicts of objectives that prevailed between managers and shareholders in view of enshrining the level of corporate governance. Similarly, Becht et al. (2005) pointed out that corporate governance regulation promoted credible commitments to higher quality governance by companies. Most importantly, Levine (1998, 1999) and La Porta et al. (2002) stated that poor legal environment coupled with weak law enforcements contributed towards inefficient resource allocation. Martynova and Renneboog (2010) developed a corporate governance index but confined to 30 European countries and the US economy. Beck et al. (2001) developed a database on political institutions worldwide though governance structures were given less prominent role than political issues.

In 2014, the Thomson Reuters launched the Corporate Responsibility Indices which constitute a suite of benchmarks geared towards assessing the performance of companies with superior ratings for Environmental, Social and Governance Practices for a large database of 4600 companies worldwide which are rated in over 225 key indicators of Environmental, Social and Governance performance. However, our methodology does not factor in the Thomson Reuters ratings since the data is expensive to get access to, let alone the fact that the coverage is mainly for the US, European companies and not central banks under three main segments, namely, Thomson Reuters CRI US Large Cap ESG, Thomson Reuters CRI Developed Markets (ex-US) ESG and Thomson Reuters CRI Europe ESG.

The current methodology incorporates the Worldwide Governance Indicators developed by the World Bank for the year 2013. In essence, estimates of the six constituting metrics are used, namely, the voice and accountability metric, rule of law metric, control of corruption metric, government effectiveness metric, political stability and absence of violence/terrorism metric and regulatory quality metric. The estimate provides the country's score on the aggregate indicator, in units of a standard normal distribution, i.e. ranging from approximately −2.5 to 2.5. The sum of these six metrics' scores is taken as values and divided by 2.5 to generate the final scores which are then adjusted to unleash markings in the range of 0–5 marks.

4.5 Generating Scores and Rankings from the Ratings Methodology

Table 4.5 provides a summarized version of the markings adopted by the ratings methodology. In all, 27 metrics are employed to trigger a holistic rating assessments of central banks in the world. The marks range from −46.75 to 110.5. Once the ratings are derived for each central bank, a ranking system is then adhered to. Central banks which obtain high marks are ranked lower (1, 2, 3,.., where 1 denotes first). Conversely, central banks which scored poorly in the ratings methodology are ranked higher on the ranking scale.

Larcker et al. (2007) built 14 governance factors by using the technique of principal component analysis. Kaplan and Urwitz (1979) focussed on statistical techniques for forecasting bond ratings. Their findings showed that Ordinary Least Squares regressions did better than probit models. Chandy and Duett (1990) rating models are based on logit, multiple discriminant analysis and recursive partitioning algorithm. However, all the above-mentioned techniques tend to be based on regression analysis to thereby differ from the current rating methodology

Table 4.5 Markings of metrics under ratings methodology

Metrics of assessment	*Marks allocated*
Staff efficiency	0 or 5
Publication of Financial Stability Report	0, 2 or 5
Consumer Price Index-Price stability	0 or 5
Language on website	0 or 5
Research Papers	0 or 5
Z-Score	−10, 0 or 5
Risk Management information	0 or 5
International accounting policy used	−5 or 0
Quality of website	0 to 10
Adherence to green concept	0 or 5
Contact information	−5 or 0
IMF above mean age	0 or 5
Notes to financial statements	0 or 5
Conferences/Workshops/Seminars	0 or 2
IMF member	0 or 5
Timely reporting	−5 or 0
Professional Accounting Firms	0 or 5
Stress Testing	0 or 5
Debt management	−5 or 0
Inflation targeting	0 or 5
Power to control money supply	−5 or 0
Central Bank Independence	0 to 5
Bank Regulation and Supervision:	−5 to 6
(i) change in the index of bank capital regulations	−3 to 3
(ii) change in the index of deposit insurance	−3.75 to 4.5
(iii) change in the index of official supervisory powers	
Global Regulatory framework for banks under Basel III	0, 2.5 or 5
Worldwide Governance Indicators	0 to 5
Total marks attributed	**−46.75 to 110.5**

which merely adopts a system of rating for central banks based on well-defined metrics. The most difficult element in any rating methodology/system pertains to the design of the weighing structure. Pensions and Investment Research Consultants Ltd (PIRC)[6] constitutes Europe's largest independent corporate governance and shareholder advisory consultancy. PIRC clings to a well-specified weighing structure when generating governance rating as follows: 17 per cent for auditing and

[6] Website: http://pirc.co.uk.

reporting rating, 25 per cent for board rating, 38 per cent for compensation/remuneration rating and 20 per cent for shareholders and capital rating. The current study attempts to generate an equal weight metric as far as possible. Both quantitative and qualitative metrics are employed and metrics are of Boolean indicators or continuous types. To be realistic and rational, certain metrics enjoy broader marks such as in the case of z-score, banking regulation and supervision and quality of central bank website. The methodology used is considered to be robust based on the use of a broad set of metrics which capture the quality of central banking worldwide, let alone focus being laid on relevance, independent information and objective measurability. We strongly believe that the ratings provide objective standards for comparison.

References

Alesina, A., & Summers, L. H. (1993). Central bank independence and macroeconomic performance: Some comparative evidence. *Journal of Money, Credit and Banking, 25*(2), 151–162.

Allayannis, G., & Weston, J. (2001). The use of foreign derivatives and firm market value. *The Review of Financial Studies, 14*(1), 243–276.

Alpanda, S., & Honig, A. (2009). The impact of central bank independence on political monetary cycles in advanced and developing nations. *Journal of Money, Credit and Banking, 41*(7), 1365–1389.

Ashbaugh-Skaife, H., Collins, D. W., & LaFond, R. (2006). The effects of corporate governance on firms' credit ratings. *Journal of Accounting and Economics, 42*, 203–243.

Backer, M., & Gosman, M. (1980). The use of financial ratios in credit downgrade decisions. *Financial Management, 9*, 53–56.

Bank for International Settlements. (2009). *Communication of monetary policy decisions by central banks: What is revealed and why* (BIS Papers No. 47).

Barro, R. J., & Gordon, D. B. (1983, August). A positive theory of monetary policy in a natural rate model. *Journal of Political Economy, 91*(4), 589–610.

Barth, J. R., Caprio, G., & Levine, R. (2013). *Bank regulation and supervision in 180 countries from 1999 to 2011* (NBER Working Papers 18733). National Bureau of Economic Research, Inc.

Basel Committee on Banking Supervision. (2009). *Principles for sound stress testing practices and supervision*. Bank for International Settlements. http://www.bis.org/publ/bcbs155.pdf

Basel Committee on Banking Supervision. (2013). http://www.bis.org/bcbs/charter.htm

Becht, M., Bolton, P., & Röell, A. (2005). *Corporate governance and control: Finance* (Working Paper No. 02/2002).

Beck, T., Demirgüç-Kunt, A., & Maksimovic, V. (2001). *Financial and legal constraints to firm growth: Does size matter?* (World Bank Policy Research Working Paper 2784).

Bernanke, B. S., Reinhart, V. R., & Sack, B. P. (2004). Monetary policy alternatives at the zero bound: An empirical assessment. Brookings Papers on Economic Activity, Economic Studies Program, *The Brookings Institution, 35*(2), 1–100.

Bertay, A. C., Demirgüç-Kunt, A., & Huizinga, H. (2013). Do we need big banks? Evidence on performance, strategy and market discipline. *Journal of Financial Intermeidation, 22*(4), 532–558.

Best, A. M. (1992). *Best's key rating guide, life health.* A.M. Best Co., Inc.

Borio, C., & Drehman, M. (2009). *Towards an operational framework for financial stability: "Fuzzy" measurement and its consequences* (BIS Working Papers No. 284).

Bowman, D., Gagnon, E., & Leahy, M. (2010). *Interest on excess reserves as a monetary policy instrument: The experience of foreign central banks* (International Finance Discussion Papers Number 996).

Brown, L., & Caylor, M. (2006). Corporate governance and firm valuation. *Journal of Accounting and Public Policy, 25*, 409–434.

Caruana, J. (2014). *The role of central banks in macroeconomic and financial stability* (BIS Paper 76).

Cecchetti, S. G. (2002, September). *Study Center Gerzensee, Newsletter.*

Cecchetti, S. G., & O'Sullivan, R. (2003). The European central bank and the federal reserve. *Oxford Review of Economic Policy, 19*(1), 30–43.

Chandy, P. R., & Duett, E. H. (1990). Commercial paper rating models. *Quarterly Journal of Business and Economics, 29*, 79–101.

Chrigui, Z., Boujelbene, Y., & Mhamdi, G. (2011). Central bank independence and inflation: Evidence from emerging countries. *Journal of Policy Modeling, 33*, 453–469.

Čihák, M., Demirgüç-Kunt, A., Feyen, E., & Levine, R. (2012). *Benchmarking financial development around the world* (World Bank Policy Research Working Paper 6175).

Cukierman, A. (1992). *Central bank strategy, credibility, and independence: Theory and evidence* (1st edn, Vol. 1). MIT Press Books, The MIT Press.

Cukierman, A., Webb, S., & Neyapti, B. (1992). Measuring the independence of central banks and its effect on policy outcomes. *The World Bank Economic Review, 6*, 353–398.

Daines, R. M., Gow, I. D., & Larcker, D. F. (2010). Rating the ratings: How good are commercial governance ratings? *Journal of Financial Economics, 98*, 439–461.

de Haan, J., Masciandaro, D., & Quintyn, M. (2008). Does central bank independence still matter? *European Journal of Political Economy, 24*, 717–721.

Demertzis, M., & Hallett, A. H. (2007). Central bank transparency in theory and practice. *Journal of Macroeconomics, 29*, 760–789.

Dincer, N., & Eichengreen, B. (2014). Central bank transparency and independence: Updates and new measures. *International Journal of Central Banking, 10*, 189–253.

Dreher, A., Sturm, J. E., & de Haan, J. (2007). *Does high inflation cause central bankers to lose their job? Evidence based on a new data set* (CESifo Working Paper No. 2045).

Dreher, A., Sturm, J. E., & de Haan, J. (2010). When is a central bank governor replaced? Evidence based on a new data set. *Journal of Macroeconomics, 32*, 766–781.

Ertugrul, M., & Hedge, S. (2009). Corporate governance ratings and firm performance. *Financial Management, 38*, 139–160.

European Financial Reporting Advisory Group. (2012). *Towards a Disclosure Framework for the Notes Discussion Paper.*

Filardo, A., Mohanty, M., & Moreno, R. (2012). *Central bank and government debt management: Issues for monetary policy* (BIS Paper 67).

Financial Sector Assessment Programs, IMF/World Bank. (2003). *Review, lessons, and issues going forward.*

Förch, T., & Sunde, U. (2012). Central bank independence and stock market returns in emerging economies. *Economic Letters, 115*, 77–80.

Gerdesmeier, D., Roffia, B., & Mongelli, F. P. (2007). The eurosystem, the U.S. federal reserve, and the Bank of Japan: Similarities and differences. *Journal of Money, Credit and Banking, 39*(7), 1785–1819.

Gompers, P., Ishii, J., & Metrick, A. (2003). Corporate governance and equity prices. *Quarterly Journal of Economics, 118*, 107–155.

Grilli, V., Masciandaro, D., & Tabellini, G. (1991). Political and monetary institutions and public financial policies in the industrial countries. *Economic Policy, 6*, 341–392.

Grossman, S. J., & Hart, O. D. (1980). Takeover bids, the free-rider problem, and the theory of the corporation. *The Bell Journal of Economics, 11*(1), 42–64.

Hale, G. (2011). *Bank relationships, business cycles, and financial crises* (NBER Working Paper No. 17356).

Hannan, T. H., & Hanweck, G. A. (1988). Bank insolvency risk and the market for large certificates of deposit. *Journal of Money Credit and Banking, 20*(2), 203–211.

Hayat, M. A., & Farvaque, E. (2012). Public attitudes towards central bank independence: Lessons from the foundation of the ECB. *European Journal of Political Economy, 28*, 512–523.

Hefeker, C., & Zimmer, B. (2011). The optimal choice of central bank independence and conservatism under uncertainty. *Journal of Macroeconomics, 33*, 595–606.

Hielscher, K., & Markwardt, G. (2012). The role of political institutions for the effectiveness of central bank independence. *European Journal of Political Economy, 28*, 286–301.

ICAP GROUP S.A. (2013). *Credit ratings assignment methodology.*

International Monetary Fund. (1999). *Code of good practices on transparency in monetary and financial policies: Declaration of principles.*

Jacome, L. I., & Vazquez, F. (2008). Is there any link between legal central bank independence and inflation? Evidence from Latin America and the Carribean. *European Journal of Political Economy, 24*, 788–801.

Jayadev, A. (2006). Differing preferences between anti-inflation and anti-unemployment policy among the rich and the poor. *Economics Letters, 91*(1), 67–71.

Jobst, A. A., Ong, L. L., & Schmieder, C. (2013). *A framework for macroprudential bank solvency stress testing: Application to S-25 and other G-20 country FSAPs* (IMF Working Paper, WP/13/68).

Kaplan, R. S., & Urwitz, G. (1979). Statistical models of bond ratings: A methodological inquiry. *The Journal of Business, 52*(2), 231–261.

King, M. (2012). *Twenty years of inflation targeting*. Bank of England. The Stamp Memorial Lecture, London School of Economics.

Kydland, F. E., & Prescott, E. C. (1977). Rules rather than discretion: The inconsistency of optimal plans. *Journal of Political Economy, 85*, 473–491.

La Porta, R., Lopez-de-Silanes, F., Shleifer, A., & Vishny, R. W. (1997). Legal determinants of external finance. *Journal of Finance, 52*(3), 1131–1150.

La Porta, R., Lopez-de-Silanes, F., Shleifer, A., & Vishny, R. W. (1998). Law and finance. *Journal of Political Economy, 106*, 1113–1155.

La Porta, R., Lopez-de-Silanes, F., Shleifer, A., & Vishny, R. W. (2002). Investor protection and corporate valuation. *Journal of Finance, 57*(3), 1147–1170.

Larcker, D., Richardson, S., & Tuna, I. (2007). Corporate governance, accounting outcomes, and organizational performance. *The Accounting Review, 82*(4), 963–1008.

Levine, R. (1998). The legal environment, banks, and long-run economic growth. *Journal of Money, Credit and Banking, 30*(3), 596–661.

Levine, R. (1999). Law, finance, and economic growth. *Journal of Financial Intermediation, 8*, 36–67.

Martynova, M., & Renneboog. L. (2010). *A corporate governance index: convergence and diversity of national corporate governance regulations center* (Discussion Paper Series No. 2010–17), pp. 1–34.

McDermott, J. (2012). *The future of inflation targeting?* BIS central bankers' speeches.

Mishkin, F. S. (2000). *Inflation targeting in emerging market countries* (NBER Working Paper Series 7618).

Miwa, Y., & Ramseyer, J. M. (2005). Who appoints them, what do they do? Evidence on outside directors from Japan. *Journal of Economics and Management Strategy, 14*, 299–336.

Morningstar Corporate Credit Rating. (2014). *Morningstar's approach to rating corporate credit.*

Nier, E. W. (2009). *Financial stability frameworks and the role of central banks: Lessons from the crisis* (International Monetary Fund, WP/09/70).

OECD. (2014). *Risk management and corporate governance, corporate governance.* OECD Publishing. https://doi.org/10.1787/9789264208636-en

Packer, F., & Tarashev, N. (2011). Rating methodologies for banks. *BIS Quarterly Review.*

Pottier, S. W. (1997). Life insurer risk characteristics and the rating process. *Journal of Insurance Issues, 20*, 111–130.

Rogoff, K. (1985). The optimal degree of commitment to an intermediate monetary target. *Quarterly Journal of Economics, 100*, 1169–1190.

Shirakawa, M. (2013). Central banking: Before, during, and after the crisis. *International Journal of Central Banking.*

Shleifer, A., & Vishny, R. W. (1986). Large shareholders and corporate control. *Journal of Political Economy, 94*(3), 461–488.

Siklos, P. (2008). No single definition of central bank independence is right for all countries. *European Journal of Political Economy, 24*, 802–816.

The Committee on the Global Financial System. (2011). *Interactions of sovereign debt management with monetary conditions and financial stability: Lessons and implications for central banks* (CGFS Papers No. 42).

The International Federation of Accountants. (2005). *Building an investment climate of trust.*

The World Bank. (2014). *World development indicators.* http://data.worldbank.org/sites/default/files/wdi-2014-book.pdf

Thomson Reuters Corporate Responsibility Ratings (TRCRR). (2013). *Rating and ranking rules and methodologies.*

Tietenberg, T. (1998). Disclosure strategies for pollution control. *Environmental and Resource Economics, 11*, 587–602.

Ueda, K., & Valencia, F. (2012). *Central bank independence and macroprudential regulation* (International Monetary Fund, WP/12/101).

UNEP Finance Initiative. (2007). *Green financial products and services.* Current Trends and Future Opportunities in North America.

Weiss, M. A. (2014, July 17). *International monetary fund: Background and issues for congress.* http://fas.org/sgp/crs/misc/R42019.pdf

Weymark, D. (2007). Inflation, government transfers, and optimal central bank independence. *European Economic Review, 51*, 297–315.

CHAPTER 5

Second and Third Division Rated Central Banks

5.1 Classification of Central Banks into Second and Third Categories

As per the Bank for International Settlement, there are 176 central banks posted under central bank websites. The European Central Bank is removed since only National Central Banks are considered based under a country-wise perspective, leaving the sample size to 175 central banks. Based on no availability of data for countries enlisted under Bank of Central African States (Cameroon, Central African Republic, Chad, Equatorial Guinea and Gabon) and Central Bank of West African States (Benin, Burkina Faso, Guinea-Bissau, Mali, Niger, Senegal and Togo), these 12 countries were thereby removed from 175, leading to a refined sample of 163 central banks. Thereafter, B-rated and C-rated central banks were removed, as depicted in Tables 5.1 and 5.2, respectively, excluding only Central Bank of West African States in Table 5.1 to obviate double counting. In all, 51 central banks were removed from 175 central banks ending up with 124 central banks. These 124 central banks were classified under excellence division as they are perceived as A-rated central banks. In the case of the US, annual reports of the Board of Governors of the Federal Reserve System are used.

In the case of Eastern Caribbean countries, the Eastern Caribbean Central Bank is used due to no access to data of its 8 countries (Anguilla, Antigua and Barbuda, Commonwealth of Dominica, Grenada,

I. Ramlall, *Central Bank Ratings*,
https://doi.org/10.1007/978-3-030-98713-8_5

Table 5.1 Second division rated central banks (Category B)

Country	*Reason*
Algeria	In French and no financials found
Bank of Central African States	Cameroon, Central African Republic, Chad, Equatorial Guinea and Gabon
Cambodia	No financial statement on annual reports
Central Bank of West African States	In French and no income statement was available for the seven countries (Congo being the exception where data was available)
China	Not all financials in the annual report
Colombia	Reports are not in English
Comoros	In French and financials not in details
Curaçao	In English but no financial reports are available
Dominican Republic	Website in English but no reports available
Egypt	No financials in the annual report
El Savador	Financials not in English
Ethiopia	No financials in annual reports
Guatemala	Website in English but no reports available
Guinea	In French and very brief financials
Hondura	Annual reports not in English
Lao People's Democratic Republic	In English but brief balance sheet present in reports with no income statements
Lebanon	Only for the year 2005 that annual report is present
Macao	Too concise information in annual reports
Mexico	Only income statements, no balance sheet present
Netherlands Antilles	No reports available
Nigeria	Only annual reports 2011 and 2012 are displayed on the website
Palestine	In English but no financials present in annual reports
Nicaragua	No reports available
Qatar	Patchy, very brief financials present in 2012 annual report
San Marino	English annual reports available only for 2011 and 2012
Saudi Arabia	Too few years and too brief information
Sudan	No financials in annual reports
Surinam	Information available in Dutch

(continued)

Table 5.1 (continued)

Country	*Reason*
Syrian Arab Republic	In English but no annual reports present
Turkmenistan	In English but no annual reports present
Vietnam	No financials for 2004 and 2009
Yemen	Not good quality

Table 5.2 Third division rated central banks (Category C)

Country	*Reason*
Angola	Home page of central bank not in English
Bolivia	Website not in English
Costa Rica	Nothing reported in English, let alone the website itself
Cuba	Web page of central bank itself is not available
Ecuador	Home page of central bank not in English
Libya	Website not in English
Paraguay	Website not in English
Uruguay	Website not in English
Venezuela	Website not in English

Montserrat, St Kitts and Nevis, Saint Lucia and St. Vincent and The Grenadines). This is the only exception where country-wise perspective is not respected but this is not an issue of concern based on countries sharing similar features, data unavailability and, let alone, only one data point in a sample of 124 units. Consequently, the 124 countries represent around 71% of all central banks in the world based on a population size of 175. The above finding clearly shows that still around 29% of central banks in the world are not able to provide proper financials to the general local and foreign audience, accentuating the concern of information asymmetries at the global level. This reminds us of the window dressings achieved by European countries just to get entry to the European Monetary Union. It can therefore be conjectured that, at the global level, information asymmetry is still looming large and that authorities need to come up with stringent measures such as mandatory reporting of all central bank financials in English with consistent and standardized accounting framework for ease of comparisons.

CHAPTER 6

Results and Discussions

6.1 Results and Discussions

The global central bank ratings are based on central banks found in the excellence division, also labelled as category A central banks, which consisted of 124 central banks relative to 114 central banks employed in the first edition. Category B central banks fail to meet certain established criteria relative to central banks enlisted in excellence division. Indeed, second division rated central banks (or category B central banks) comprise all those central banks which failed to furnish full versions of their financial statements. Moreover, in spite of the fact that a central bank may provide full version of its financials, it is imperative to ensure a sufficient flow of information, i.e. there is no break in the availability of financial statements. For example, a break is noted in 2004 and 2009 in the case of the Central Bank of Vietnam when it comes to financial reporting. As a prerequisite condition, all central banks found in this bucket of classification should be having their websites in any of the two international languages-English or French. Another factor for making central banks found in category B pertains to the absence of financials in either English or French language.

Overall, 42 central banks in the world are found in category B and 9 central banks in category C. Category C exclusively considers central banks which fail to have their websites either in English or French. Interestingly, most of the countries found in category C emanates from either North or South American continents with two countries hailing from

I. Ramlall, *Central Bank Ratings*,
https://doi.org/10.1007/978-3-030-98713-8_6

the African continent, namely Angola and Libya. Most of the data end as of December 2017/2018 with the financials extended to December 2017/2018, depending on data availability.

Negative markings have been assigned in the case of the following categories, namely, negative z-score values, no recourse towards any international accounting policy, absence of any easy contact details, fulfilling debt management tasks, impotency with respect to control in money supply and late reporting. The purpose for the negative markings is to cater certain malpractices which go against the principle of sound central banking and which spawn higher propensity of hampering on their crucial role. For instance, by involving itself in the debt management task, a central bank is susceptible to undertake measures that can impede on the transparency in the conduct of monetary policy. In the same vein, late reporting induces scepticism with respect to the quality of information disseminated, let alone ability to initiate proactive actions. For instance, as of January 2022, the latest annual report for Central Bank of Greece happened to be still its annual report for the year 2019. Lack of power to control money supply considerably undermines the power of a central bank in performing its task of price stability. Negative z-score sends signals of a poorly capitalized central bank which can trigger the question of viability of policies envisaged. Poor contact details inhibit the free flow of information between a central bank and the outside general public, significantly declining the credibility of monetary policy.

6.2 Rankings

Figures 6.1, 6.2 and 6.3 illustrate the final rankings for each of the central banks classified in excellence division. The top ten list comprises central banks from the following countries, namely France (1st place), Italy (2nd place), Canada (3rd place), New Zealand (4th place), Belgium (5th place), Sweden (6th place), The Netherlands (7th place), Switzerland (8th place), UK (9th place) and Australia (10th place).

Alike the ratings obtained in the first edition, there is clear evidence that European central banks predominate the top 10 list of the best central banks in the world. Coupled with the latter, there is clear evidence that advanced economies have the best central banks in the world. France tops the list as the number one central bank in the world. This can be attributed to a myriad of qualitative reasons. First, France is considered as a second-powered horse behind Germany in the European Monetary

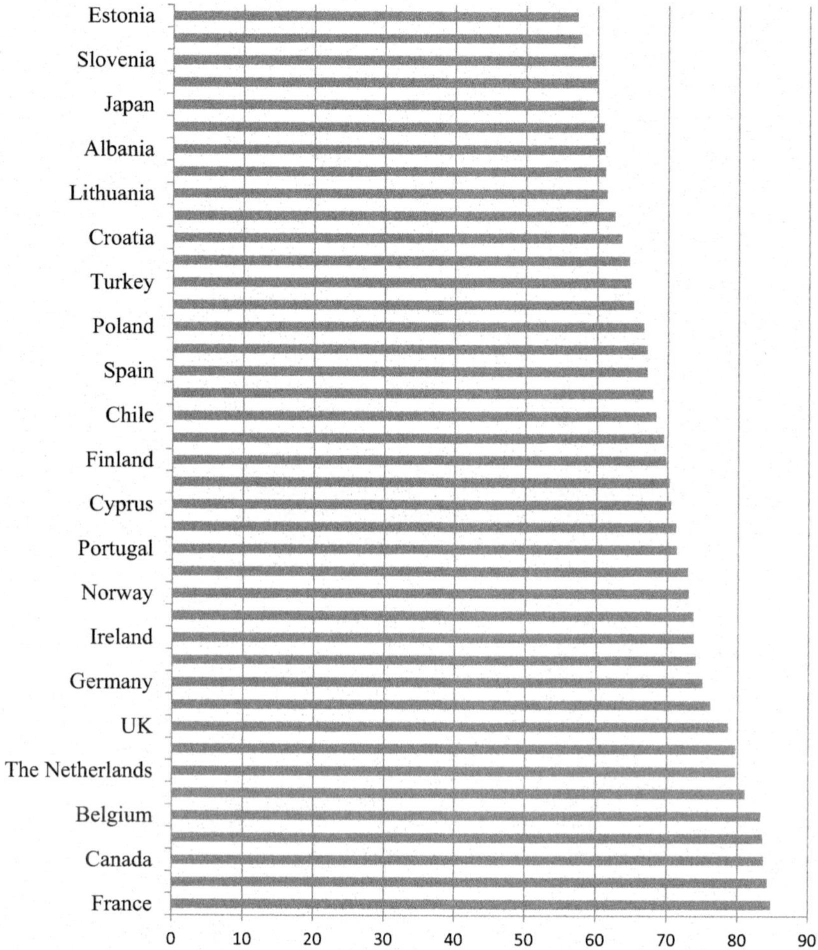

Fig. 6.1 Marks—Upper batch

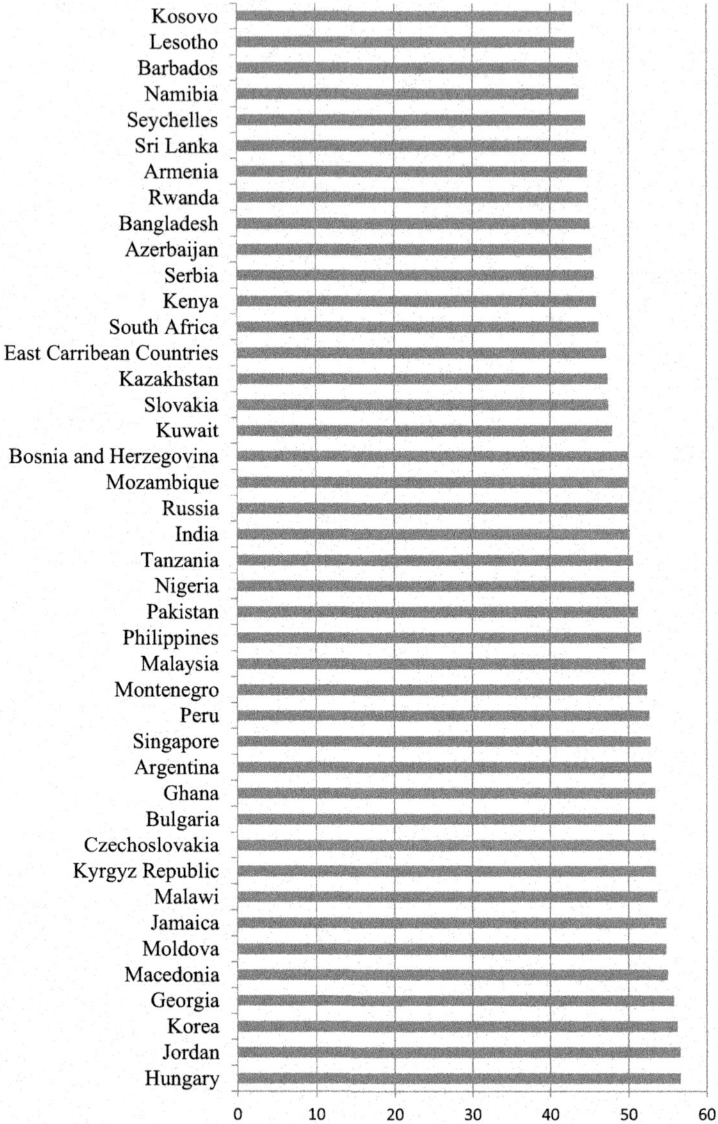

Fig. 6.2 Marks—Middle batch

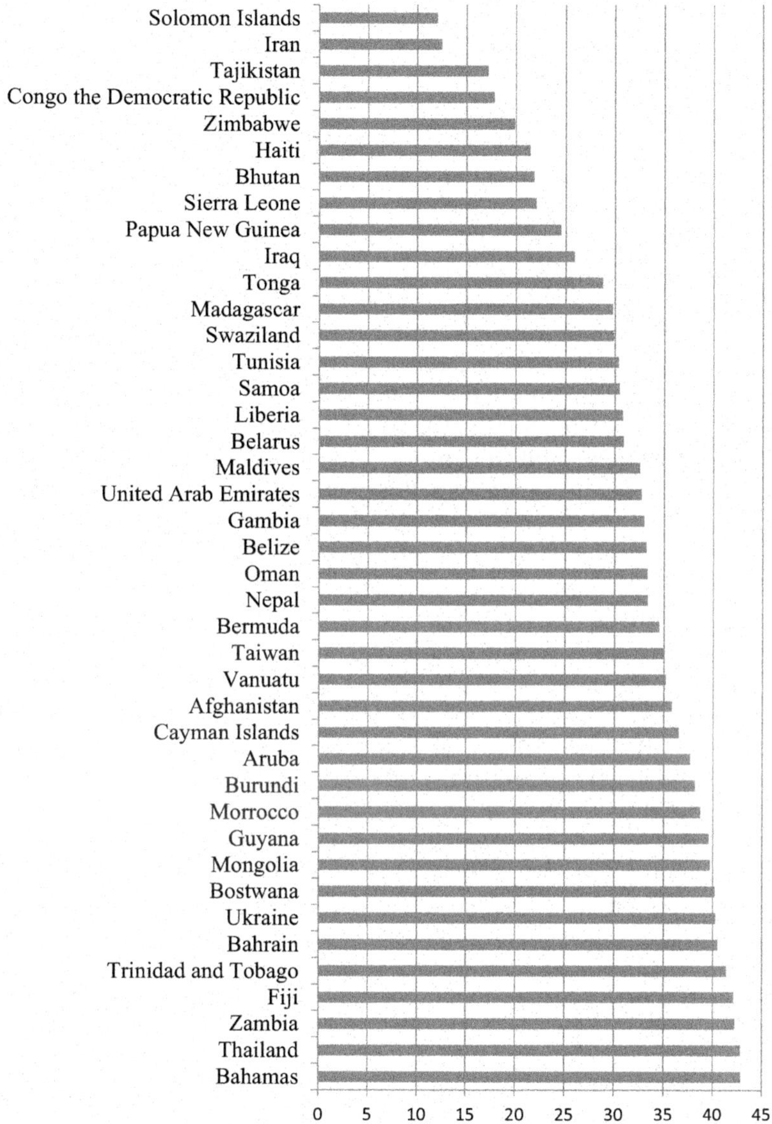

Fig. 6.3 Marks—Lower batch

Union. Second, the Banque de France is a leader in terms of green finance among various central banks in the world under Network for Greening the Financial System (NGFS). Relatedly, Banque de France endorses responsible investment by stimulating the growth of sustainable finance. Third, Banque de France is widely considered as a leader in technological advancement as put forward by Central Banking.[1] Last but not least, Banque de France is widely perceived as a pioneer in Central Bank Digital Currencies when it comes to central banking.

The central bank of Canada retained its supremacy among the top five banks in the world by emerging out as the third top-rated central bank based on the score obtained. Such a finding bolters the fact that Canada remains as one of the coveted countries in the world in terms of maintained economic activities. The Central Bank of Canada is also a member of NGFS, likewise the National Bank of Belgium which emerged out at the fifth place. The ranked position of the National Bank of Belgium could be explained by positive spillover effects as France is very close to Belgium.

The Bank of England is usually considered as a model in central banking in the world. One of the major forces of the Bank of England pertains to its ability to wield its money supply as and when required compared to countries which adopted the euro. In terms of research, there has always been a constant motivation to always seek high-quality research in distinct areas of central banking. The bank also rejoices over the best quality website along with the central bank of Chile, the only two central banks which harnessed the maximum marks under website quality.

Interestingly, our new list of top 10 central banks consists of two central banks emanating from Pacific Ocean, namely, Reserve Bank of Australia and the Reserve Bank of New Zealand. It is no wonder to central bankers that the Reserve Bank of New Zealand constitutes a widely admired central bank as being the pioneer in the sphere of inflation targeting which is now considered as a key ingredient of monetary policy around the world, with its philosophy being ingrained in the Maastricht Treaty.

The Swiss National Bank also demonstrates state of art tools and techniques in the field of central banks. Above all, strong economic fundamentals also buttress our derived ratings. For instance, Switzerland is

[1] https://www.centralbanking.com/fintech/4397586/pioneer-award-banque-de-france.

widely coveted worldwide as the best place to retire. The Swiss National Bank is also a pioneer in Central Bank Digital Currencies. Sveriges Riksbank ranked sixth among the top ten banks in the world. It is no wonder that the central bank of Sweden has established itself as a leader in central banking, bearing in mind that it is and will remain the oldest central bank in the world. As a matter of fact, our ratings obtained tend to favour eldest banks in the world. A quick glance at Fig. 3.6 from Chapter 3 clearly reveals that Sweden, UK, France and The Netherlands among the top eldest central banks in the world.

6.3 Metrics Under Discussion

The current section discusses the results under each of the 27 metrics under consideration.

6.3.1 Research

Around 84 per cent of the central banks undertake research on a regular basis based on above-median number of research papers. Research encompasses working papers, discussion papers and research papers. There is thus now stronger stamina for central banks to undertake research as this is the basis for sound decision-making processes. Just like a portfolio manager needs to cushion himself from actions taken in portfolio management, a central banker also protects himself by justifying the course of policies taken through backed research results. In a nutshell, there is significant evidence that many central banks are now directly involved in research. Such a finding bodes well with the fact that research should be a constant and regular feature of central banks in an attempt to generate better insight on monetary policy, financial stability, financial inclusion and risk management. The Federal Reserve Bank of the US clearly demarcates from all central banks based on its highest and well-diverse number of research papers published. In general, African countries are found to be lagging behind European countries. It can be conjectured that research tends to be a rather vital component of central banks found in advanced economies which can afford to recruit the best researchers while central banks found in less advanced economies tend to relegate research to the second order. It could also be that research is done but not widely reported in the case of less advanced economies but that could be something counterintuitive as communicated research to the general public may ironically enshrine the credibility element of monetary policy strategies deployed. The advent of research is that it not only assists in sieving out areas of vulnerabilities to initiate proactive measures for improvement but also in setting a platform whereby distinct central banks can muster their efforts to leverage on the quality of central banking worldwide to enshrine global financial stability. Moreover, research assists in proper modelling to ensure that sound policies are taken in lieu of mere intuitive thinking not endorsed by any solid econometric model.

6.3.2 Conferences/Workshops/Seminars

About 88 per cent of central banks in undertake conferences, workshops and seminars with the information available on their respective websites. There is growing commitment among central bankers to be involved in these activities as part of their policies in bolstering the level of communication to the general public. This can positively be linked to the rising level among central banks which now go hand in hand with the organizations of conferences, workshops and seminars. Promulgation of research should therefore improve on these activities. The regular organizations of conferences/workshops/seminars tend to permeate central banks in view of fostering regular international collaborations to further unleash positive momentum to conferences, workshops and seminars, let alone inspiring high-quality deliberations on burning issues, as and when required, such as Central Bank Digital Currencies have now taken robust grips on the research agenda of nearly all central banks in the world.

6.3.3 Financial Stability Reports

Despite the fact that the global financial crisis of 2007–2008 triggered vigour in the publication of financial stability reports among central banks in the world, yet, not all central banks publish these reports. Sometimes, different appellations are used. For instance, in the case of Bhutan, they called it Financial Sector Performance Review. Only 74 per cent of the sample publishes financial stability reports. It is anticipated that COVID-19 will unleash further boost to the publication of financial stability reports in the world. For example, the latest report available for the central Bank of Greece remains at the year 2010 as at end of 2014 but with the emergence of COVID-19, the latest report issued was based on the year 2021 as at the start of 2022. As part of its implicit objective in safeguarding the financial stability of a country, it is imperative to ensure that financial stability reports constitute an inherent publication policy of all central banks in the world. Most importantly, there is a pressing need for a platform to ensure that financial stability reports are comparable across different countries. Again, the Bank for International Settlement can be mandated to establish the minimum level of information and presentation quality of financial stability reports. As a matter of fact, the veracity of information reported should be checked with an external party to ascertain that no bias prevails. Moreover, to promote research, it would be advisable that a financial stability database is set up on the website of each central bank such as financial soundness indicators, something which is already conspicuous for some central banks. Stated differently, some central banks have already built such a database.

6.3.4 *Late Reporting*

One of the cruxes in financial statements reporting relates to timely availability of information. In fact, it utterly defeats the purpose of preparing financial statements for a given year if the latter happens to be a stale year such as two years post the recommended year. The ultimate aim underlying timely reporting refers to ability to use such information to improve future activities. Most importantly, late reporting is symptomatic to weak discipline and responsibility which automatically undermines the credibility of a central bank. Iran, Haiti, Zimbabwe, Tajikistan, Vanuatu, Gambia, Congo, Iraq, Afghanistan and Cayman Islands have been identified as the top ten late reporters. Overall, most central banks in the world ensure timely reporting of their annual reports, showing committed efforts towards timely availability of information. It can be conjectured that, in general, central banks adhere to good quality reporting based on the critical role that they play in the world.

6.3.5 *Green Implementation*

Merely 33 out of 124 central banks cling to green implementation as stipulated in their respective annual reports. The Reserve Bank of Australia established proper metrics of assessments with respect to the environmental impacts of its policies. Consumption of electricity, gas, water and paper are regularly monitored to ensure efficiency in the use of materials. Moreover, strenuous efforts have been made to ensure that fuel efficiency stays within the Australian Government's green guidelines for vehicle fleets with around 52 per cent of the waste generated by the bank being recycled.

The central bank of Austria (Oesterreichische Nationalbank) was awarded the Austrian Eco-Management and Audit Scheme (EMAS) Prize in 2012. The EMAS constitutes a voluntary environmental management instrument designed by the European Commission to enable organizations to continuously enshrine their environmental performance. The central bank of Austria (OeNB) participated in the EMAS scheme since 1999, showing its continued adherence towards environmental protection.

The central bank of Brazil (Banco Central Do Brasil) undertook considerable efforts in greening its activities. Technical specifications of IT equipment are examined to ensure a maximum level of recycling possibility. Besides, its headquarters under construction in Rio de Janeiro has been assigned green building certification under Leadership in Energy and Environmental Design.

The central bank of Canada initiated safer, cheaper and greener notes production, unique among world's currencies. The central bank of Cayman Islands has a Green initiative programme of recycling aluminium products and newspapers.

The Bank of England Head office building obtained the Corporation of London's Clean City Gold award for waste management in 2010 based on more than 99 per cent of its waste being recycled. Moreover, the bank reduces its environmental impact through energy-efficient equipment and improved waste management. The bank's publications are done using paper which consists of 50 per cent recovered waste and 50 per cent virgin fibre.

The central bank of France stimulates research on low carbon sustainable growth. Besides, it defined an Environmental Footprint Reduction Master Plan based under five principal components: scaling down energy consumption, increase the share of renewable energy in the energy mix, reducing water consumption and optimizing employee travel and enhancing energy performance at real estate and IT level.

The Hong Kong Monetary Authority has over 50 per cent of its paper consumption emanating from recycled paper. Moreover, the staffs of Hong Kong Monetary Authority are actively involved in campaigns to collect toys, computers and other reusable materials which are then given as donations to charities.

The central bank of Hungary (Magyar Nemzeti Bank), accredited with Eco-Management and Audit Scheme in 2011, is constantly involved in activities aimed at reducing its environmental burdens. Operations were rationalized, LED lights used modernization of the lighting system to decrease energy consumption. Moreover, the green activities undertaken at the bank have helped to reduce carbon emissions by nearly 10 per cent in the lapse of two years. Other activities include introduction of water-saving technological solutions, optimizing on the fleet of printers and photocopiers and planning forward for green procurements. The bank has also won the title as a bicycle-friendly workplace based on a higher number of its employees cycling to work.

The Reserve Bank of India has undertaken important steps such as removals of old air conditioner to be replaced by energy-efficient ones. Most importantly, the bank has already commissioned for green rating under the Leadership in Energy and Environment Design-Existing Building.

The central bank of Jamaica stated its continued efforts to further green the bank on the back of mustered actions towards operational efficiency and undertaking environmental awareness programmes worldwide.

The central bank of the Netherlands (De Nederlandsche Bank) undertook steps to green its activities. The bank obtained ISO 14001-certified for three departments involved in environmental care with the stated aim of scaling down its carbon emissions by 50 per cent in 2013 compared to the baseline year 2007. In addition, care has been taken from procurement to disposal of ICT items to foster a greener environment. In 2012, Athon Car Lease was selected by the bank with respect to its fleet of vehicle to foster greener activities under a green lease policy framework.

The central bank of Norway (Norges Bank) initiated green activities such as reduction of power consumption, establishing efficient management of light and ventilation systems and efficient long-term building maintenance, setting green standards with respect to procurement of goods and services and management of office waste.

The Central bank of Switzerland (Swiss National Bank) publishes an environmental report, showing its unrelenting commitment to reduce its environmental impacts. Besides, two of the bank's buildings are heated solely through lake water in lieu of natural gas. Furthermore, more than 50 per cent of its natural gas is used being derived from biogas.

The central bank of Barbados undertook strong commitment towards green activities by entitling its annual report 2011 under the theme "Towards a Green Economy". The bank greened its information technology processes in view of scaling down energy usage. The central bank of Malaysia (Bank Negara Malaysia) conducted seminars on projects related to Green Technology Financing Scheme in 2011.

The central bank of Greece regularly publishes information pertaining to Greenhouse Gas emissions for EU and Greece in its annual reports, depicting a heightened level of information dissemination to sensitize people towards greener activities.

6.3.6 IMF Membership

IMF membership confers positive benefits to member countries. Such a state of affairs has been magnified in light of the crisis through general and special SDR allocations. Moreover, IMF membership trails behind reinforced quality in implementation of tasks such as technical assistance, econometric modelling and quality research. Furthermore, IMF member countries tend to collaborate among themselves at regional and international levels in the sphere of conferences, seminars and research in needy areas such as financial stability and consolidation of the banking system in light of the recent crisis. All central banks found in category A are members of IMF with the exception of Aruba, Bermuda, Cayman Islands, Hong Kong and Taiwan. Most countries in the world are now members of the IMF due to positive benefits that such membership confers to them. Technical and financial assistance during critical times and knowledge building tend to be major benefits that accrue to member countries.

6.3.7 Contact Information

With the advent of technology, emails constitute the easiest, quickest and practically costless way of sending and receiving information worldwide. Effective transmission of communication calls for bi-directional flow of communication from the central bank to outsiders and vice versa. Ukraine does not provide contact details via an email address on its website. Such deterrence to communication blatantly goes against the principle of sound central banking which should, de facto, promotes regular bi-directional flow of information between a central bank and the general public. It can be deduced that central bank of Ukraine is not so much concerned about public opinion on their decisions and feedbacks on their reports and activities. Besides, absence of emails fosters a rather opaque approach to operations.

6.3.8 Accounting Policy Used

The quality of financials rests a lot on the accounting policy applied. Quality and transparency-conscious central banks resort towards quality policies such as US GAAP, IFRS and ECB guidelines. Should there be no information unleashed about the accounting policy used, then, this sends a strong signal of a poor quality information processing level. The central banks of the following countries do not provide information on their accounting policy used, namely, Bahrain, Belarus, Bhutan, Iceland, Iran, Japan, Kuwait and Taiwan. This shortcoming calls for an international body that would look into a consistent and standard accounting policy for the reporting of central bank financials. The rest of the central banks mostly fall under ECB guidelines, IFRS and US GAAP accounting policies, respectively.

6.3.9 Negative Z-Score Central Banks

Though a central bank constitutes the only financial institution in the world that can operate under negative equity, yet, poor equity base tends to jeopardize the credibility and transparency of monetary policy on the back of low independence level. Negative z-score values are found for central banks in the following countries, namely, Tajikistan, Slovakia, Israel, Czechoslovakia, Thailand, Chile and Belarus, among others. These central banks are penalized via negative markings. Negative equity undermines the ability of a central bank to perform its mandatory functions. For instance, if a country is subject to a situation whereby public debt has already breached its threshold as to initiate mounting pressures to curtail expenditures, then, its central bank will try to mitigate costs. The latter may hamper on effective sterilization operations geared to shun off undesired inflationary pressures. Finally, poor financial health may constrain the ability of a central bank to undertake major projects likely to reinvigorate the quality of central banking such as issuance of safer and greener banking notes.

6.3.10 Staff Efficiency

Staff costs constitute an important component for central banks in the world. The average staff costs per employee is computed over the period 2000 to 2017–2018 for all central banks. Then, the median value is derived. Overall, 45 central banks have their staff costs level below the median value for all central banks in category A, representing around 36 per cent of the sample. All central banks report their staff costs in their financial statements except in the case of Bostwana, India, Korea, Malaysia and Taiwan. In these cases, no marks are assigned as absence of staff costs information most probably signifies excessive costs borne under staff expenses. The benefit of such a metric is that it lays out a yardstick for central banks to exert control on their operating costs so that efficiency is strived.

6.3.11 Risk Management

Risks constitute an inherent feature of any institution in the world. Not all central banks divulge details of their risk management tasks-a flaw in reporting that should be tackled through an imposed set of rules and procedures. Merely 49 per cent of central banks enlisted in category A undertake full reporting of their risk management situations. A priori, from the perspective of central banking, it can be argued that risks are not susceptible to trigger considerable impacts on bottom line of central banks in the world. Central banks are usually characterized by well-controlled and manageable risks levels. However, there is a need to have standard reporting requirements to ease comparisons. For instance, while most central banks adhere to net asset exposure under currency risks, some central banks resort towards gross asset exposures. Such a divergence in reporting is likely to buffet international comparisons. Technically speaking, liquidity does not pose important risks to a central bank based on its sole notes and coins issuance power. Nonetheless, excessive exploitation of this printing press power can generate inflation, let alone transparency highly required to anchor inflationary expectations and thereby ensure an effective monetary policy transmission mechanism. In the same vein, currency risk exposures constitute an inherent risk component of central banks in view of their mandated foreign reserve management tasks. Geographical credit risk concentrations are not widely reported but represent important vectors of country risk exposures. A vital element for dissemination of the above risks metrics relates to the scope for research enhancement in the area of central banking such as gauging the impact of the crisis on central bank risk management.

6.3.12 Inflation Targeting

The reference guide is http://www.centralbanknews.info/p/inflation-targets.html for central banks adhering to inflation targeting, updated list as of 2020. Implicit inflation targeting countries are catered in by focussing on all euro area members in the sample. In some cases, there have been ramifications, i.e. drift from explicit to implicit inflation targeting. For instance, due to the adoption of the euro, Finland, Slovakia and Spain abandoned their respective inflation-targeting frameworks, as they need to adhere to the Maastricht convergence criteria on inflation. Overall, around 58 per cent of the central banks found in category A are inflation targeters-whether implicitly or explicitly, depicting committed efforts towards price stability.

6.3.13 Notes to the Accounts

Financial statements are usually elaborated via notes to the accounts which provide information on specific items to enhance insight of the readers. In essence, financial statements not fully endorsed by notes to the accounts, fail to convey the right information to outsiders. For example, detailed information on operating expenses helps to know the major sources of costs borne by a central bank. A central bank which does not furnish notes to its financials could feasibly signal undermined transparency, accountability and responsibility with possibilities of window dressings. Hopefully, around 87 per cent (108 central banks out of 124) of the central banks found in category A provide notes to their financials which is commendable. However, still, bearing in mind the critical function played by central banks, it is important to have a full reporting of all vital information, including full dissemination of notes to the accounts. In terms of policies, this could herald the need of an international body that would ensure minimum reporting of notes to the accounts.

6.3.14 *Quality of Website*

Factoring key ingredients such as attractiveness, uniqueness, quality of the data retrieval system, comprehensiveness of information reported and general display of information, marks are assigned with respect to each central bank's website quality. Only two central banks obtain full marks, namely the Bank of England and Central Bank of Chile based on their outstanding website quality, sophisticated data retrieval system, comprehensive display of information and well-co-ordinated activities. The minimum marks allocated are 3 points which are given to the central banks found in Afghanistan, Bahamas, Bermuda and Samoa based on their very poor quality of website, let alone no major database with respect to vital monetary and economic statistics.

6.3.15 *Stress Testing*

Stress testing exercises represent vital risk assessment tools wielded by many institutions worldwide in view of distilling down key areas of vulnerabilities that would eventually demand proactive risk management procedures. Ninety-two out of 124 central banks report information on stress testing, showing off the need for sound risk management at the global level. Unfortunately, the quality of information on stress testing disseminated differs across distinct countries. In the case of Czechoslovakia, there is an extensive and in-depth analysis of stress testing information displayed separately on its website. In other cases, just few paragraphs are reported on stress testing. This could set the stage for an internationally standardized reporting framework for stress testing for all central banks in the world. This becomes critically important with respect to the scenarios to be applied, the econometric model to be calibrated and the distinct risks level to be ingrained in the stress testing framework.

6.3.16 *Languages Used*

The quality of communication undertaken heavily hinges on the type of language used. More than one language used would be useful in increasing the level of understanding of policies envisaged by a central bank to its outside public. Single language use is unlikely to be much useful since most countries cling to English as their official language with a different language deemed as their local language. It can be argued that countries which have their local languages already in English, single language dissemination would be sufficient. Nonetheless, these countries could further improve their communication process via use of international languages. Hence, the criteria of two languages in information dissemination appear well adapted. The rationale is that one language pertains to local language dissemination and another language for foreign language dissemination. But, in the case of Australia, Bermuda, Cayman Islands, UK and the US, positive marks are allocated since the English language constitutes the spoken language in these countries.

6.3.17 Debt Management

Debt management constitutes a complex activity that usually overlaps between monetary policy and fiscal policy. As a sound and transparent central bank, it is imperative that debt management tasks are undertaken outside the premises or do not fall under the purview of functions of a central bank to ensure to the maximum possible level that there are no manipulative forces that may thwart on the effective implementation of monetary policy. Around 6.5 per cent of central banks in category A mixes up monetary policy function with the presence of debt management. There is still a need to review the activities of these central banks under the establishment of a well-designed framework to delineate debt management function from monetary policy function, cleansing down monetary policy activities from any feasible infringement.

6.3.18 Professional Accounting Body

Ninety-eight out of 124 central banks have recourse towards professional accounting bodies when preparing their financial statements. KPMG, Deloitte & Touche, Pricewaterhousecoopers, Ernst & Young and Grant Thornton, in decreasing order of significance, are selected preferences by central banks in the world. KPMG is the most widely employed accounting body with a hefty participation rate. Such a finding can also signify that KPMG is the most strategically placed accounting body as it has access to financials of most central banks in the world. There could be bouts of strategic information access as to its own benefits. For instance, by knowing the investment strategies of major central banks whose investment actions can significantly influence international assets prices, it becomes easier to muster all these information and filter down the general trend of asset prices. By availing of such information, these accounting firms can attempt to generate own profits. Unfortunately, nothing as such has been established in the world with respect to the level of critical information accessed by accounting firms on central bank financials. However, based on the more or less well-spread selection of accounting firms among central banks, such information asymmetry is susceptible to be of minor significance. Nonetheless, if an accounting firm has access to critical financials of major central banks (amount in lieu of number), this can pose potential risks of strategic information use to make bonanza.

6.3.19 IMF Age Membership

Using the median IMF age membership as the cut-off level, central banks, in which their countries have their membership age above that of the median IMF age membership level, are assigned five marks. Overall, 71 central banks are positively rated. The reason for such a state of affairs relates to better and mature countries which have availed a longer period of financial and technical assistance from the IMF which thereby trigger positive impacts on their operational activities. This is akin to the concept of relationship banking but here at the international level. Longer period of relationship established with IMF tends to generate enhanced level of central banking activities, all likely to consolidate the health of the global financial system.

6.3.20 Consumer Price Index (CPI)

One of the major objectives of any central bank pertains to maintenance of price stability. Such an aim helps to bolster confidence which is a key ingredient to grease the sands of the economic wheels. Low price levels definitely assist in inducing higher confidence level. Using the median value of CPI for all central banks as the cut-off value, positive marks are assigned in the case of very low CPI levels below the median value. Seventy-six out of 124 central banks are positively rated. This finding signifies almost 61 per cent of the countries have high and low inflation rates, mostly attributable to the quality of the financial system. Developed countries tend to avail of low inflation rates, most likely spurred under their inflation-targeting frameworks while developing countries adhere towards higher inflation rates in view of less developed financial markets, higher bouts of imported inflation and higher interest rates to motivate higher capital inflows, usually required to finance their mounting levels of current account deficits elicited via higher imports.

6.3.21 *Power to Control Money Supply*

The power to control money supply is directly tributary to the exchange rate system adopted in a country. Indeed, under fixed exchange rate systems, central banks are not able to easily control the money supply. Countries forming part of the eurozone area, Southern African Customs Union (excluding South Africa) and those adopting currency boards are negatively rated.

6.3.22 *Central Bank Independence*

Kyrgyz Republic ranked itself first while India was ranked lowest as per zero marks attributed. Since the marking is done for all countries present in the original sample, a slight trailing effect is noted in that our selected sample of countries has its lowest-rated central bank rated as from 0.79 in lieu of 0.

Because not all countries had their data present under the central bank metric (CBIW) of Dincer and Eichengreen (2014), a vacuum was left and which needed to be filled. For instance, Denmark and Switzerland did not contain their respective CBIW data. In that respect, a proxy is used, namely, the central bank transparency from the same researchers to shun off any feasible bias in the ratings/ranking system. The data values for the proxy ranged from 0 to 13.5 and adjustments were made to derive values in range of 0–5 for the various countries. In the extreme cases of absence of any data for countries like Gambia, Haiti, Kosovo, Madagascar, Montenegro, Nepal and Serbia, nil marks are assigned.

6.3.23 *Bank Regulation and Supervision (3 Metrics)*

Bank regulation and supervision constitutes a preponderant component in the financial system of any country in the world. In fact, it is widely considered that sound bank regulation and supervision constitutes an important ingredient in safeguarding the financial stability of banking systems worldwide. Based on the fact that not all central banks are directly involved in the supervisory tasks, it becomes important to level the playing field by incorporating metrics of bank regulation and supervision. The three components are as follows: change in the index of bank capital regulations (−5 to 6), change in the index of official supervisory power (−3.75 to 4.5) and change in the index of deposit insurance (−3 to 3), all based on Survey I to IV from the study of Barth et al. (2013).

Under deposit insurance, the ultimate objective is geared towards enactment of sound deposit insurance schemes to obviate the occurrence of systemic crises. Croatia emerged as the best country while Oman posted the worst performance. Many countries (81 in all) scored nil marks, plainly showing that over the years 1999–2011, not much changes have occurred in the area of deposit insurance schemes by virtue of the fact that the index measures the change in the deposit insurance regime over time. In the case of official supervisory power, the aim is to gauge on the extent of power availed by the regulatory body to initiate changes as and when required. Results show that Seychelles made considerable progress in terms of substantially leveraging the power of its regulatory body while Kazakhstan bottomed the list. Finally, under bank capital regulations, Bangladesh and Turkey topped the list while Austria and England registered the worst performances. The worst performances of Austria and England is due to the fact that both countries scaled down the stringency of capital regulations following the US subprime crisis.

6.3.24 Global Regulatory Framework for Banks Under Basel III

Using the data published from the Bank for International Settlements with respect to the progress report pertaining to the status of adoption of Basel III, Australia, Canada, South Africa, Hong Kong SAR, India, Japan, Singapore and Switzerland scored the maximum marks on the back of completion of Basle III adoption. Belgium, Brazil, UK, the US, France, Germany, Indonesia, Italy, Korea, Luxembourg, The Netherlands, Russia, Spain, Sweden and Turkey scored half marks based on their still in progress approach to Basel III adoption. The rest of the countries scored nil marks.

6.3.25 Worldwide Governance Indicators

Sound governance is sine qua non for proper functioning of any institution. Based on the use of country ratings, it becomes considerate to have recourse towards worldwide governance indicators to reflect the level of governance status ingrained in each country under consideration. Finland conspicuously demarcates itself as the winner based on its adherence to robust principles of governance structures while Afghanistan situates itself at the other end of the continuum. Other countries are also found in the upper rungs of the rating ladder, namely, Switzerland, Sweden, Singapore, Norway, New Zealand, The Netherlands, Luxembourg, Iceland, Germany, Denmark, Canada, Austria and Australia. In general, it can be conjectured that mainly advanced economies tend to be imbued with robust governance structures.

References

Barth, J. R., Caprio, G., & Levine, R. (2013). *Bank regulation and supervision in 180 countries from 1999 to 2011* (NBER Working Papers 18733). National Bureau of Economic Research.

Dincer, N., & Eichengreen, B. (2014). Central bank transparency and independence: Updates and new measures. *International Journal of Central Banking, 10*, 189–253.

CHAPTER 7

Backtesting

7.1 Backtesting

Any developed ratings should be rigorously assessed to confirm their validity, more precisely, to confirm their reliability in use. This requires the use of external data sources in the validation process. To fulfil that requirement, recourse is made to the following data, namely, Ease of Doing Business, Human Development Index and Corruption Perception Index and Sovereign ratings data. Correlation coefficient analysis is employed in the verification process. A more robust estimation technique is also being considered in our analysis, namely, quantile regressions to sieve out whether the causality of the relationship differs at different levels of the data.

Overall, there is robust evidence that the developed central bank rankings approach befits with already established country indices, making it an interesting and innovative way to relook at the features of countries. Most importantly, the quality of central banks appears to be an important driver in accounting for ease of doing business, human development level, the corruption level and sovereign ratings. This could provide a vigour in the use of central bank rankings at a worldwide level whenever gauging the characteristics of countries. Above all, the central bank rankings approach can be made dynamic through yearly review to sieve out any major changes at countries level.

I. Ramlall, *Central Bank Ratings*,
https://doi.org/10.1007/978-3-030-98713-8_7

7.2 Backtesting: Validation of the Central Bank Rankings with Other International Rankings

The newly developed central bank ratings/rankings are scrutinized to assess their validity. In practice, any developed index/rating should be examined to gauge its validity prior to its effective application. The best avenue employed to undertake such a task is to resort to already established and internationally coveted metrics. To generate a solid background for analysis, recourse is made towards three world rankings, namely Ease of Doing Business May 2019, Human Development Index 2018 and Corruption Perception Index 2018. Based on the fact that the central bank ratings data end as of 2018, an attempt is made to find data as close as possible to 2018 to ensure quality in our backtesting analysis. However, data for sovereign ratings and 10-year CDS spreads were obtained for the years 2022 and 2020, respectively.[1] Technically speaking, correlation coefficients are widely used to investigate the extent of association among distinct variables. A too low correlation coefficient would be synonymous with a low level of association, reducing the power of the newly developed rankings. Conversely, a too high correlation coefficient value would dissipate the need for the new rankings as the already present variable constitutes its best proxy. Beyond that, a high correlation value could render dubious the quality of the newly developed rankings. Nonetheless, a fairly good level of association should subsist between the created rankings and each of the three existing international rankings. The reason is that higher quality central banks are anticipated to rejoice over enhanced ratings in terms of better ease of doing business, better human development index and lower corruption level. A priori, correlation coefficients in the range of 0.4–0.7 (or −0.4 to −0.7 in the case of negative relationship) would constitute the best values to validate the newly developed ratings/rankings.

Since data are not available for Aruba, Bermuda, Cayman Islands, East Carribean Countries and Swaziland under Ease of Doing Business, they were omitted from the sample. As can be seen in Fig. 7.1, a positive association prevails between Ease of Doing Business and Central Bank rankings under a correlation coefficient value of 0.65. Such a finding implies that countries that enjoy higher quality central banks tend to be

[1] Such data was gleaned from the following website: https://pages.stern.nyu.edu/~adamodar/New_Home_Page/datafile/ctryprem.html.

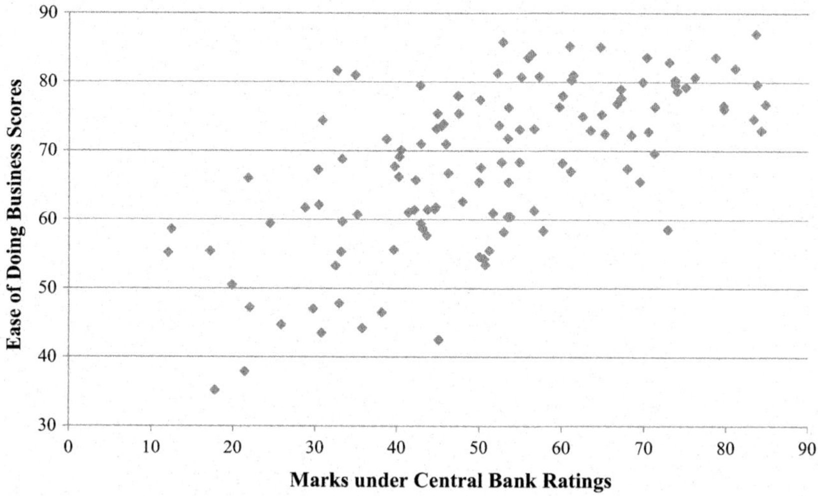

Fig. 7.1 Backtesting based on Ease of Doing Business 2019

imbued with the best conducive business atmosphere that would boost the creation of new businesses.

Swaziland, Bermuda, Taiwan, Cayman Islands, Aruba, Kosovo and East Caribbean Countries do not have data counterparts under Human Development Index. They were thereby overlooked from the sample. As depicted in Fig. 7.2, it is plain that a positive association manifests between Human Development Index and central bank rankings. The computed correlation coefficient stands at 0.68, adding robustness to the validity of the newly developed global central bank rankings. Such a result implies that countries which are endowed with higher quality central banks tend to rejoice over a much higher level of human development level, or vice versa. This further means that high-quality institutions demand high-quality human capital, as substantiated by the positive and fairly high correlation coefficient.

As demonstrated in Fig. 7.3, a positive relationship occurs between central bank rankings and the Corruption Perception Index under a correlation coefficient of 0.65. This result further corroborates the fact that the developed central bank rankings are undeniably a good measure of the quality of central banks worldwide. Under Corruption Perception Index, there is strong evidence that countries endowed with high-quality central

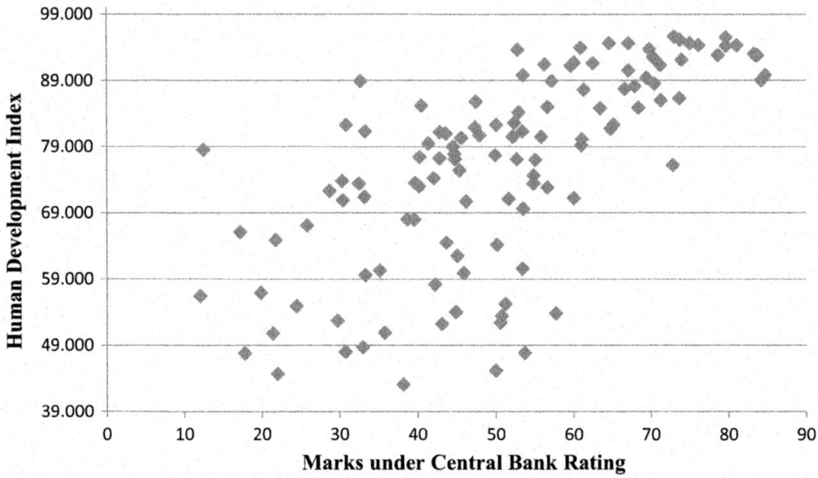

Fig. 7.2 Backtesting based on Human Development Index 2018

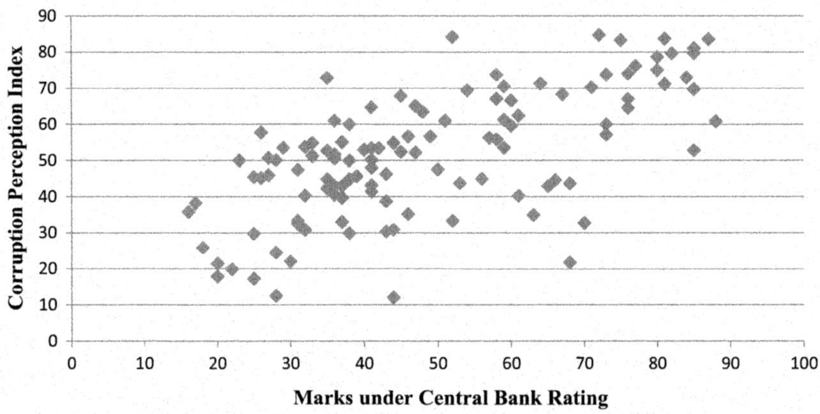

Fig. 7.3 Backtesting based on Corruption Perception Index 2018

banks tend to be less hampered by corruption problems. Stated differently, the positive correlation coefficient value clearly confirms the fact that countries that score high markets under their respective central banks, tend to also score high marks under the Corruption Perception Index. To synchronize the number of countries between the two data sets, namely, the central bank ratings' dataset and the Corruption Perception Index dataset, eight central banks (Tonga, Samoa, Belize, Bermuda, Cayman Islands, Aruba, Fiji and East Caribbean countries) had to be removed from the central bank ratings' dataset, leading to a final sample of 117 central banks.

In a nutshell, irrespective of the metric of comparison, there is robust evidence that the developed central bank rankings are powerful and reliable when gauging the quality of central banks in the world.

7.3 Sovereign Ratings and Central Bank Rankings

Sovereign ratings comprise values as shown in Table 4.1 in Chapter 4. The correlation coefficient obtained hovers around 0.60, indicative of the fact that countries that avail of higher marks under central bank ratings tend to obtain higher marks under sovereign ratings. Higher sovereign ratings' marks denote better country conditions while higher central bank marks denote enhanced central bank quality. Hence, the positive relationship, as depicted in Fig. 7.4, bodes well with the fact that countries that are endowed with high-quality central banks tend to score higher marks under Standard and Poor sovereign ratings.

7.4 Regression-Based Analysis of Central Bank Ratings

Quantile regression analysis (25th, 50th, 75th and 95th quantile values) is used to analyse the impact of central bank ratings on the ease of doing business. Marks were used for both data sets to obtain the regression coefficients. As demonstrated in Table 7.1, central bank ratings do exert a positive influence on ease of doing business with the effects gradually decreasing as the quantile level is being scaled up. All in all, for 25th, 50th and 75th quantile levels, the positive effects are not only economically significant but also statistically significant at the one per cent significance level. All in all, our finding robustly confirms the positive impact of central bank quality in enhancing the business climate in different countries of the world.

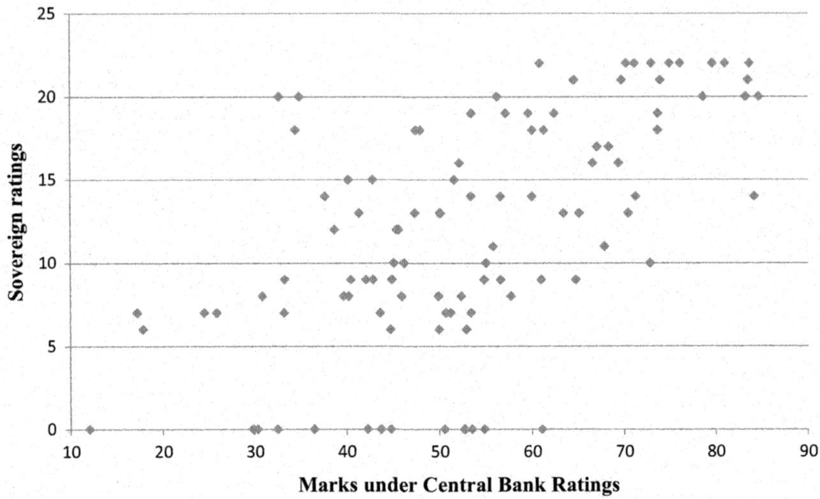

Fig. 7.4 Backtesting based on Sovereign ratings[2]

Table 7.1 Ease of Doing Business and CBR

Dependent variable				
Ease of Doing Business				
	(1)	*(2)*	*(3)*	*(4)*
CBR	0.508***	0.411***	0.340***	0.123
	(0.083)	(0.062)	(0.062)	(0.082)
Constant	36.007***	48.330***	56.893***	76.695***
	(5.011)	(3.720)	(4.053)	(4.691)
Observations	119	119	119	119

Note *$p<0.1$; **$p<0.05$; ***$p<0.01$

The analysis between central bank ratings and sovereign ratings is based on marks from these two data sources. Table 7.2 plainly shows that central bank ratings unleash positive effects on sovereign ratings at the one per

[2] Source: Standard and Poor's website.

Table 7.2 Sovereign ratings and CBR

Dependent variable				
Sovereign ratings				
	(1)	*(2)*	*(3)*	*(4)*
CBR	0.338***	0.279***	0.247***	0.104***
	(0.061)	(0.044)	(0.043)	(0.035)
Constant	−10.083***	−2.279	2.761	14.416***
	(3.515)	(2.782)	(2.805)	(2.461)
Observations	104	104	104	104

Note *p<0.1; **p<0.05; ***p<0.01

Table 7.3 10-year CDS spreads and CBR

Dependent variable				
CDS spreads				
	(1)	*(2)*	*(3)*	*(4)*
CBR	−0.0003***	−0.0005***	−0.001**	−0.003
	(0.0001)	(0.0001)	(0.0004)	(0.002)
Constant	0.022***	0.039***	0.081***	0.223
	(0.005)	(0.010)	(0.026)	(0.175)
Observations	62	62	62	62

Note *p<0.1; **p<0.05; ***p<0.01

cent significance level with the impacts gradually decreasing as the quantile level is being adjusted upwards. Similar to findings under Ease of Doing Business, the impact is of a higher magnitude in the first quantile. Our analysis corroborates the link between central bank quality (as captured by central bank ratings) and country risk level (as captured by sovereign ratings).

Though of low economic side effects, yet, the influence of central bank ratings on CDS spreads is statistically significant at the first three quantile levels, as depicted in Table 7.3.

All in all, the regression-based analyses add lustre to the correlation coefficient results, spurting out momentum to the fact that the newly developed central bank rankings do bode well with worldly reputed metrics, mainly, in the case of Ease of Doing Business and Sovereign ratings. Consequently, there is robust evidence that the developed central bank rankings are consistent with already developed key international benchmarks established to gauge the strengths of distinct countries at the global level.

CHAPTER 8

Conclusion

8.1 Summary of Global Central Bank Ratings

In light of the 2007 US Subprime crisis, strenuous efforts were exerted on the global financial system in view of mitigating systemic risks, which tend to be particularly acute for developed countries based on their high level of integrated financial systems . Central banks' interventions during the global financial crisis were critical to safeguard financial stability. A more or less similar state of affairs occurred during COVID-19 as central banks resorted once again to asset purchase programmes to ensure that economies do not lapse into recessions. All in all, the significance of central banks can never be denied. With the emergence of central bank digital currencies, the future role of central banks is further expected to be challenging and demanding. However, to date, excluding the work of Ramlall (2015), no other work has been undertaken to assess the quality of central banks in the world. This work extends the work of Ramlall (2015) by bringing forth a re-assessment of the quality of central bank ratings for the period 2017/2018. All in all, findings further bolster the ratings methodology clung by Ramlall (2015) with respect to the new time period considered for the ratings. In fact, the ratings system used is not only comprehensive but also effective as it provides due consideration to important aspects like staff efficiency, promulgation of green concepts, timely reporting of reports, among others. This book addresses these shortcomings by developing a unique 27 metrics ratings system for central

I. Ramlall, *Central Bank Ratings*,
https://doi.org/10.1007/978-3-030-98713-8_8

banks in the world. Findings show that central banks worldwide differ in terms of the activities with those from developed countries being more tilted towards consistent publications of research papers, among other types of differences. Most importantly, the ratings developed, are found to be compatible with major global indices such as Ease of Doing Business, Sovereign Ratings and Corruption Perception Index. To that effect, international authorities can use the developed ratings system to deal with weaknesses at global financial institutions levels, let alone, gaining insight as to country risk levels.

8.2 Major Shortcomings to Be Addressed by Global Authorities

While developing the ratings system, the author noted the prevalence of many flaws which buffet the global financial systems. First and foremost, there is still not a consistent reporting framework for central banks in the world. Central banks are deemed as the hearts of financial systems based on their supervisory roles. Unfortunately, international authorities have failed to create a general financial accounting system that would ensure consistent and comparable reporting of central banks. In addition, risk management information tends to be a major hurdle as not all central banks report such type of information. Second, it is imperative that financial reports are available in at least one of the two widely recognized international languages, namely English and French. Unfortunately, many central banks still publish their annual reports in their own mother tongue language only. Ironically, these central banks could be the subject of scrutiny by international authorities to ensure that there are no malpractices in reporting, let alone no elements of window dressings. Third, based on their critical roles, it is recommended that central banks should provide a detailed version of their respective financial statements in form of endorsed notes to the accounts. The underlying rationale is that, as of date, many central banks, still adhere to brief versions of financial statements. This type of reporting may ironically induce window dressing and malpractices when it comes to transparency and adherence to sound corporate governance practices. Alternatively stated, it is a pity in this century to note that the information asymmetry of Akerloff (1970) is still permeating despite the advancement of technology, available at a cheaper cost. In a nutshell, findings call for an international authority that would see to it that central banks report their financial statements on a timely basis with detailed notes to the accounts and with the information being comparable to other countries in the world. It is an irony that, the absence of such detailed reporting along with proper notes, represents a key lacunae today bearing in mind that, central banks are finally accountable to the general public based on the notion that the management of public's money requires maintenance of trust from the public.

The best way to define the crucial roles played by central banks may be akin to the statement: "Tell me your central bank, I tell you your country risk level". This could be actually the new dimension exposed by the developed ratings system based on its relationship with country sovereign ratings.

8.3 Policy Implications

One of the major implications of the current findings is that there is a need to set up an international body to bring forth a heightened level of congruity, consistency and transparency in reporting of central bank financials. Most importantly, there is a need to establish minimum reporting requirements so that vital information is disseminated to every stakeholder. The Bank for International Settlements could be mandated to fulfil such a task bearing in mind its crucial role at the global level. Overall, the following areas need to be improved.

1. Full version reporting of financial statements either in English or French version. To further enhance information dissemination, for all those central banks that cling to French reporting, they should also report in English.
2. Same accounting policies should be adopted to ease comparisons and also induce a greater level of transparency to outsiders. This could be a real hard nut to crack bearing in mind that two predominating accounting systems in the world, namely, US GAAP and IFRS.
3. Financial reports should be made available on a timely and regular basis; should there be late reporting exceeding one year, then a financial charge should be made applicable as deterrence. As a matter of fact, central banks are accountable to the general public at the end of the day and hence timely reporting of information is crucial from that perspective.

4. There should be full disclosures and consistency in reporting on risk management issues. For instance, net exposures should be reported to gauge the real extent of exposures assumed by central banks for the various types of risks.
5. It is of paramount significance to come up with a professional accounting body to cater to financial reporting of central banks to ensure that there is no critical access of such information to private accounting bodies which may avail of "herd behaviour" information about the investment strategies of central banks. Indeed, in any country, central banks are endowed with the role of foreign exchange and reserve management so that their actions can have a significant influence on global financial markets. A trader who can anticipate the herd behaviour is likely to pocket significant profits. In that respect, private accounting bodies which prepare central bank financials tend to have access to such critical information at the broader level so much so that they can easily know the investment strategies of central banks and avail of such information to their own benefit.

8.4 Main Use of Global Central Bank Ratings

The major advent of this work on central bank ratings is that the effectiveness of a central bank governor tenure can be gauged via the proposed set of metrics—creating an objective way to assess a governor freed from any political interventions. Indeed, in the case of a new governor who undertakes positive changes to improve the central bank system, the latter will definitely be reflected in the ratings adopted. Most importantly, the current work sets the pace for an international benchmark that can be used whenever assessing central bank quality. With time, the ratings metrics can be enlarged and further consolidated, for instance, the present work is based on data for the period 2017/2018 which improves on the original work which was based on data spanning the period 2012/2013. The developed global central bank ratings system is expected to be widely used by policymakers throughout the world. An award prize can be related to these ratings on a yearly or bi-annual basis to generate continued improvement on all central banks in the world—rekindling dynamic and unrelenting vigour towards excellence.

References

Akerloff, G. G. (1970). The market for 'lemons': Quality uncertainty and the market mechanism. *The Quarterly Journal of Economics, 84*(3), 488–500.

Ramlall, I. (2015). *Central bank ratings: A new methodology for global excellence.* Palgrave Macmillan.

Index

I. Ramlall, *Central Bank Ratings*, https://doi.org/10.1007/978-3-030-98713-8